"Well-written case histories are probably the most fascinating stories a person can read. . . . Abraham Schmitt, perfecting the art of story-telling, gives us the opportunity to look into his patient's lives as they reach despair and travel back to normal existence."
—*Eternity*

"After the recent barrage of writings by Christian behaviorists who are primarily concerned with changing outward appearances, it is refreshing to find a restatement of Christ's emphasis on first changing the inner man. . . . For the lay counselor, the minister, the teacher, listening with love is a powerful tool."
—*Moody Monthly*

"I found myself translating the art of listening with love to my interactions with my family, students, friends, and colleagues. . . . Listening with love is really a lifestyle for people who care. And in a very special and necessary way, it is a lifestyle for Christians."
—*Christian Home and School*

THE ART OF LISTENING WITH LOVE

Abraham Schmitt

WORD BOOKS
PUBLISHER
WACO, TEXAS

First Printing—January 1978
First Paperback Printing—May 1979

The Art of Listening with Love

Copyright © 1977, by Word Incorporated, Waco, Texas. All rights reserved. No part of this book may be reproduced in any form whatsoever, except for brief quotations in reviews, without written permission from the publisher.

Scripture quotations marked RSV are from the Revised Standard Version of the Bible, copyright 1946, 1956 and © 1971, 1973 by the Division of Christian Education of the National Council of the Churches of Christ in the United States of America, used by permission; quotations marked TLB are from *The Living Bible, Paraphrased* (Wheaton: Tyndale House Publishers, 1971) and are used by permission.

ISBN 0-8499-2883-4

Library of Congress Catalog Card Number: 77-83296

Printed in the United States of America

CONTENTS

1. JOANNE:
   Listening with Love Is Contagious 17

2. MONTFORD:
   In Which I Listen to Myself 37

3. KATHY:
   A Child Is Crying and No One Is Listening. 51

4. JIM and LINDA:
   *The Cry of Adolescents in the
   Identity Crisis.* 87

5. JOE:
   Who Listens to Thrown-Away Mates? . . . 109

6. MELISSA:
   *The Voice of a Sharecropper
   in Graduate School* 129

7. ALBERT:
   A Life That Might Have Been Heard . . . 147

8. CINDY:
   When Listening with Love Transforms . . 158

ACKNOWLEDGMENTS

To my wife, Dorothy, goes a special "thank you" for both the contents and style of this book on listening. It was she who often heard my life's message clearer than I did and then helped me respond to it accurately. Listening carefully to each other and to the relationship was the key to our marriage. As she edited and typed the manuscript, she listened to what I was intending to say and then made alterations because she already knew what to listen for. At times, after struggling in vain to shape a chapter to fit the rest, she rejected it and sent it back to me. Those chapters are rightfully not in the book. That is listening with love.

Our children have affirmed that the thesis of this book works for family living. They have responded to being heard and are now listening to their lives, each in her or his own way: Mary Lou and Ruth Ann in college, David Dean and Lois Lynn in junior high school.

To Ruth E. Smalley, Professor Emeritus and former Dean of the School of Social Work, University of Pennsylvania, I am indebted, for she exemplified in the classroom a listening lifestyle which transformed me.

To the staff of Word Books, especially Floyd W. Thatcher, Vice President and Executive Editor, I am grateful for hearing me "the listener" between the lines while they were publishing my first book *Dialogue*

With Death. Out of that experience and their encouragement this book was born.

I also wish to thank the clients and other persons whose journals and lives form the structure around which this book is written. In all cases the names and identifying material are disguised.

Abraham Schmitt, D.S.W.
Souderton, Pennsylvania

INTRODUCTION

The purpose of this book is to teach the art which I call "listening with love." This is a very special kind of listening. The word love defines it. By "listening with love" I mean that one cares so much for another person that the full depth of that person's being is heard. This is an act of love. The ultimate welfare of the other person becomes the listener's final concern. This is also my definition of love.

Listening can be done for one's own sake. We do this all the time, and it frequently has its own value. We listen to a lecture or a sermon not for the speaker's sake but for our own. This is listening, but it is not the type of listening I am attempting to teach in this book.

There is also a destructive form of listening. This type is most extreme when we gain information from someone and then use it against the person in the form of labeling or, maybe, in the form of gossip. This is using the words of another for the purpose of character assassination. Perhaps I should call this type "listening with hate."

It so happens that most people are very cautious with their speech, in that they carefully test the listener's motive before they will reveal any important data. If they do not trust or do not know the listener's intentions, they will simply relate trivia. This safeguards the speaker. Unfortunately most interpersonal relationships have such a high degree of uncertainty or mistrust in them that shallow, insignificant speech is all that is shared. And this is the case regardless of how desperately people are yearning to share, or how deeply they are hurting. It is simply not safe to do otherwise. That is exactly why a new art-form of interpersonal relationship is needed. What I mean by this I wish to communicate by using the term, "Listening with Love."

When this art is practiced it becomes a powerful means to transform people and relationships. The person who listens with love can become ultimately effective, instrumental in effecting change in the lives of other human beings. And he can then free them from the bondage of fear in relating to others, by inviting them to tell the secrets of their hearts, with the full confidence that nothing else will be done with these secrets than what is best for them. The highest good is that the listener will admire the speaker even more than ever before. He has revealed his distinctive uniqueness, and at that level one can do nothing else but adore him. Thus, his personhood must be declared "good."

To listen this way one must participate with the other in the process. It is not enough simply to stare at him silently with ears open. The other needs to know at all times that one is hearing at that very moment. The best use of this kind of listening, of course, is to free the speaker to search deeper and deeper for a more full understanding and admiration of himself. Listening is then a great act of love at that moment, for it makes the other person more whole.

That listening with love transforms is the message that this book intends to communicate at all times. Every case illustration is a person with a vital message that needs to be heard. At times it is accurately heard,

INTRODUCTION

even far beyond the speaker's expectation, and the transforming power of love breaks through and creates its own miracle. At times it might have been heard, but was not.

Let's not minimize the miraculous. I believe that we can so learn the skill of relationship—and listening is its most powerful attribute—that lives are drastically changed in our presence. This will give life its ultimate meaning, for both persons involved, each having, at that moment, discovered the final reason for existing—to help others become more whole and to be made more whole. That transforming power is given to each person to use.

Unfortunately, most of my illustrations come from professional helping settings, since that is where I spend so much of my life. But this also has an advantage in that it can better illustrate the effectiveness of the art. It was in this setting that I gained the conviction that the key skill of counseling and therapy is listening. However, it is not the private property of the professional. It belongs to everyone and can be used by everyone in all interpersonal relationships. For me, it has spread to all areas of existence. It works wherever I bump into people, and when I am not in any distinctive role. I now call "listening with love" a lifestyle for caring people and, in a special way, for Christians.

One key discovery I have made is that to listen one must know a lot about an individual and the life situations that individual has been in, is in at the time, and expects to be in. For this reason I have included a variety of dilemmas and then attempted to help the reader understand that each one calls for special knowledge, as well as a particular type of sensitivity. To be defined mentally ill is a different life predicament than to be in the throes of an adolescent crisis. Each has its own message. The voice of the hurting person has to be heard in the scream of the voiceless-voice of that life experience. The more one knows about the person, the more one can accurately hear.

The fact that there is similarity in certain ages and stages of life, and in certain situations does not make the experiences of people uniform. Each person is a unique individual and thus experiences these situations distinctively. To really hear him, his own experience, no matter how different from others, is the most essential thing to strive for. Herein each individual is unique, even though much of his message may have a familiar ring.

Early in my professional practice I would often respond to clients with the statements, "Oh! I know just what you mean," or "I know what it feels like." Later I noticed that uncomfortable silences frequently followed statements like that. It was not until I faced a black student who was pouring out his agony of the "black experience" in the classroom that I discovered the shallowness of it. I used one of those standard responses, and he snapped back, "No, you don't know what it feels like. At best I can give you only a glimpse of what it feels like. You have never worn your difference on your face like I have and been rejected because of it. Don't say you understand; just tell me you're trying to, and give me the assurance you are listening." I was responding with cliches, and my response conveyed that I failed to comprehend the uniqueness of the student. If that distinctiveness was not heard, I really wasn't listening, and what I did hear was distorted by my life experience.

In this book I have often selected illustrations of the

INTRODUCTION

weakest, the poorest, and the most devastated people. My reason for doing this is that I want the reader to respond to them. They, too, have their story to tell, though they are least listened to. People with prestige, power, or wealth will find their listeners. Success brings with it an audience that will listen, but love listens to the least heard in our midst.

My central motive for writing this book is to define the highest form of love in a way that the average reader can practice it effectively. Love has been so confused in our society that it is revolting even to think of it as it is usually portrayed. Yet love is what humanity craves. If it is an integral part of unselfish listening, then love becomes wholesome again. I believe this is why Jesus called "Love your neighbor as yourself" the greatest commandment. May I add, "Listen with love to your neighbor even as you listen lovingly to yourself."

There is a developmental sequence to the chapters of this book. In the first chapter I use the case of Joanne, primarily because it so dramatically illustrates how clearly the voice of a so-called "mentally ill" person in a state hospital can be heard. When Joanne was responded to, the effect spread through her to her children and even to the hospital staff. The act of listening with love is contagious.

Momentarily, I pause in chapter 2 to have the reader know me. I am as unique as I say everyone else is. I discovered this when people who cared helped me listen to myself. I hear many messages when I listen to myself; I have shared a few of these. The purpose of this chapter is to convey that a true listener must listen to himself with love before he can listen to others. If one's own cry jams the receiving set, another's cry will not be heard.

In chapter 3 I go to the beginning of the developmental phases. Children need to be heard. Though their words may be simple and clear, they likely are saying much more symbolically. Their total lives may speak the pain that family members inflict upon each other. At times what children don't say is more important to hear than what they do say; in chapter 3 Kathy will be crying for many of her peers.

Adolescence is a painful period for communication, as chapter 4 illustrates. Psychologically, adolescents need to create distance from their parents and from other adults to complete the most important phase of the entire developmental process. So, how can we listen when they really aren't saying much to us? It's difficult, to say the least. Maybe it is best to say that we need to understand the stage of development. Then we can know that they don't mean for us to believe what they are screaming literally. What they aren't saying may be the most important message. This, too, can be understood.

In chapter 5 I turn to the message of marriage. Here I let the despairing cry of a mate who has been thrown away communicate the message. My reason for using this example is that there are so many of these persons in our midst, and if anyone needs to be heard, they do.

Melissa, in chapter 6, illustrates how much the situations of life affect the message. She is carrying in her psyche the scars of her people. To love the minority we need to hear the anguish of the past as well as the present. It is to the situations of people that I ask you to listen sensitively.

I move on to older adults in chapter 7. One needs to

INTRODUCTION

tune in to the past experiences of older people and the hope—or hopelessness—of the future. Time is running out for them. No drastic changes can be made any more. Then, with little time left, what must we listen for? Let Albert speak to us.

That love transforms what it loves is the message of the final chapter. When the lonely cry of Cindy was heard, she came out of hiding in her "haunted house" and mingled with mankind. She was indeed a new person.

The transforming power of love has been a part of me throughout my adult life. At first I knew it only in theological terms. It was the divine love of God, expressed perfectly in the sacrificial gift of his son to mankind. This was the ultimate in unselfishness since it led to the final test of love—Jesus Christ's being willing to die for the sake of mankind. In his own words, "Greater love has no man than this, that a man lay down his life for his friends" (John 15:13, RSV).

It was not until I entered the University of Pennsylvania's School of Social Work that this profound theological truth was translated, for me, into interpersonal practice. Love, regardless of whether it is expressed by God or by man, transforms what it loves. Initially this was dramatically demonstrated by the faculty toward me as a person. Someone cared about my every act, my every feeling, my every motive. The more I shared, the more they responded in affirmation. They seemed to hear every utterance of my soul. As a result I emerged a transformed human being. This is exactly what unconditional love does—it transforms. It asks nothing in return but that you would accept it and then go practice it with others.

It was at this time that I found an obscure article by

Paul Tillich wherein he relates this self-sacrificing love to the art of listening.* Following this I discovered a new directive for life. It was simply to listen with love and individuals would be transformed. The key to all my professional practice was to tune in on the lives of people sensitively, in whatever way was appropriate to my function.

Now, almost twenty years later, I have an accumulation of illustrations and a depth of conviction that must be shared. My hope is that this will inspire others to hear the call to listen sensitively to the hurts of humanity and discover the healing power of listening.

---

* "The Philosophy of Social Work," *The Social Service Review*, 36, no. 1 (March, 1962):13–16.

1

JOANNE
*Listening with Love
Is Contagious*

"Joanne Smith is a twenty-eight-year old separated, Protestant, white female housewife admitted to the State Hospital for ninety days from the county prison.

"The commitment papers state that this woman freely admits stabbing her mother many times with an ice pick. She says she has always fought with her mother, but that she didn't mean to hurt her. She feels as if she is going to die. She feels that this is necessary because of what she did to her mother. She is now quite depressed and remorseful. When seen in prison she had a black eye and some scratch marks on her arm."

I became overwhelmed as I read these words on the referral sheet from the admitting doctor to me, the social worker assigned to "take a history on this case." This must be case number twenty-five that I am now handling, I thought. How can I take on one more, especially this one? The need is so desperate. They are all so extreme; otherwise, they don't come to a state hospital.

But then, this is the price I pay for being on the social service staff of a hospital like this. It is filled with thousands of human misfits. The back wards are crawling with the chronic cases who receive no help. "Society's scrap heap" is what someone has called them. One more admission to the heap and I am supposed to do something, now, after all else has failed for years and years.

How can I care for these people in here? Long ago, when they could have been helped, no one did. Then, why now?

I knew this was no mindset for visiting a new patient for the first time. But I, too, have an endurance limit. This added another case to my already overwhelming load, and when one is already overwhelmed with work, any addition feels only like a burden.

Slowly I walked across the campus to the admissions building of a Maryland State Hospital. The admission ward, on the female side, is really gruesome—dozens and dozens of way-out human beings, milling around the huge day room like a herd of crazy cattle. They are all newly "psychotic, totally out of touch with reality." So the records say; otherwise, they wouldn't be here. Some are screaming at the top of their lungs. Others are carrying on highly animated conversation with delusional persons on the TV set. Some sit motionless on the floor, heads between their knees, in deep depression. It is out of this crowd that I had to find Mrs. Joanne Smith, as my slip of paper said.

With the help of an attendant I soon found her sitting alone on her bed in the dormitory wing. Dressed in the white denimlike gowns, they all look alike. I only noted that she was young, very thin, and small. Her hair was totally disheveled. She was weeping silently as we approached—in total despair!

How, in heaven's name, can I care for her?" I groaned inwardly. She was immediately startled when I sat beside her and told her I was a social worker as-

JOANNE: *Listening with Love Is Contagious*

signed to her, to help her use the hospital services in whatever way I could.

Her first question was, did I think she would ever get out of here. She had several relatives who had ended up in state hospitals, where they eventually died. I could only say that I did not know, especially since she was committed by a court order on a felony charge. My assignment at this time was to get a complete case history to help the hospital decide on the course of treatment.

She then told her story:

"In our family if you're in trouble you're alone. My life is like a tangled knotted grapevine fifty years old. To be as young as I am, I'm messed up all over. I can think a lot better now, though, than I could before. I hacked up my mother because things built up to such a point I just couldn't stand it anymore. I'm sorry for what I did. I still love my mother.

"My family has always been poor. I was made to live with several families as I grew up because there was never enough for all the children to eat. I am the youngest and I never felt that I was wanted. My mother lived in a shack. Father left the family when I was a baby and we have never seen him since. Even as a child I had to work for people in return for food. At fifteen I got married to a fellow who was eighteen just to get away from my mother. I already was pregnant then, but the baby died because it was defective. We lived with my husband's parents because my husband thought I needed to be trained by them. He used to go out every night, even dated other women. To me, he said, 'I took you out of the trash, what more do you expect?' He finally left to live with another woman. I will always love him, but the other woman has got him now. We had another baby together. He is now eleven years old.

"I married again at twenty-four years of age. Two children now three and four were born in quick succession. I didn't know it but my husband had a long record of sexual perversion. When he sexually assaulted my children and the children in the neighborhood, I couldn't let it go on any longer, so I had to call the police and testify against him. He was sent to a state prison on an indefinite sentence. That means until he is cured. How could he ever be cured? So, he remains there forever.

"After this I got an apartment together with my mother and my three children. We lived on public assistance. My son was terribly confused by what my husband did to him sexually, so for a long while he had to see a child psychiatrist. I also went to a family agency, but they didn't know what to do for me. They told me that my problems of keeping the family alive were so great that I didn't have the energy to do anything about my emotional problems.

"Life in our apartment was hectic from the beginning. I never did get along with my mother. She needed to control everybody, including the children and me, like she did when we were small. I ran away to get married the first time just to be free from her. So here I was raising my children without a father, like I was raised. And to think that these children's father was in prison, possibly for life, just because I turned him in. All of this became too much for me. I had no one to turn to, so I sought the help of a spiritual advisor. She told me that my mother was possessed of the devil, and ought to be gotten rid of. When I stabbed her, that is exactly what I thought I ought to be doing."

JOANNE: *Listening with Love Is Contagious* 21

I sat in stark amazement as I heard this frail little woman tell her story. She was caught in a terrible dilemma far beyond human tolerance. She was not an example of the frailty of man, but an example of the sheer fortitude of man that is determined to exist against all odds. A psychotic break was the natural end product of her situation.

I returned to my office to write the history for the psychiatric staff. I was determined to show how devastating life had been for this woman—that anything and everything she had done was out of sheer desperation after life had crumbled. My mind repeatedly returned to Victor Frankl and his victorious survival in death camp as he so beautifully tells it in *Man's Search for Meaning*.* But he, at least, could identify his enemy; Mrs. Smith could not. Her courage was equal to his, I thought. I would have to convince this hospital to give her a chance in life, the one she had never had.

A few months later Mrs. Smith appeared for a psychiatric staff conference. First, the history I had prepared was read in its entirety. I sensed a genuine aura of reverence in the room. They had heard my message. Soon Mrs. Smith was brought into the room. She looked very frail and extremely scared; I had the feeling that as far as she was concerned this was her murder trial. Her responses were weak and barely audible. She accepted blame for everything and threw herself at the mercy of the court.

After she was led from the room the superintendent of the hospital turned to me to ask for my evaluation. First, I asked that the patient be assigned to me be-

---

* (New York: Washington Square Press, 1963).

cause she needed help so desperately and because I wanted to help her. I suggested that she not be returned to court but kept at the hospital, that the court should be notified to delay her hearing until we could prove the incident was due to an inevitable psychotic break. Then, after we could show she was fully recovered, we could ask the court to drop the charges. I believed her chances for recovery were excellent. She had proved this throughout her life. Finally, I asked the staff's permission to arrange an immediate get-together with her children. It was Christmas and I didn't think the family should spend it divided. Besides, the children had all witnessed the brutal attack on the grandmother. They needed to see their mother so as to cope with all their frightening feelings.

The eyes of the superintendent welled up as she gazed at me and said, "Every one of your recommendations is accepted. Go ahead; plan for the family visit immediately. We will take care of the official details later. I'm sure there are no funds for Christmas gifts for these children. Could you let me know later what is appropriate? I will purchase them myself if no other source is available. Next patient, please."

In no time the visit was planned. The Children's Bureau which had custody of the children agreed to gather them from their foster homes and transport them to the hospital. Never before had such a visit been held here, but the social service lounge was quickly transformed into a visit site, with a Christmas tree, decorations, and gifts from the superintendent and various staff members. One senior social worker even baked cookies; in her mind Christmas required it.

Why all this caring? I soon realized that caring is a contagious process. Once I had listened to the real hurt cry of a devastated human being and responded appropriately to that hurt, a whole host of people also heard. This happened in the midst of such overwhelming need—thousands of patients who each had their own story to tell, staff members who were already extending themselves to their human limits. And yet there was all this available for one more patient. I was simply touched by this pathetic situation that had systematically destroyed a human being. Once I allowed myself to respond to this desperate need, it swept a whole department and many others with it. That is simply beautiful! And just to think, had I made my history taking only routine, as I could so easily have done—after all, there are at least a dozen new admissions every week—then I would have lost this profound experience.

Listening with love is contagious, I now concluded. My colleagues were all infected by it. Yet I hadn't asked them to get involved. They couldn't help it. Once they heard the cry of one person, they responded. They heard because I heard.

A few days after the staff conference I stopped to see Mrs. Smith at the admissions building. She could not remember me from the initial interview; as she put it, "I was so terribly sick then." But she did remember seeing me at the staffing. Suddenly she became extremely apprehensive as she asked, "Did I make staff?" I knew what she meant. "To make staff" is a patient definition of being discharged. I was shocked that her doctor hadn't told her. He was at the conference. Days had passed and no one had made the effort to tell her, when such an important decision had been made about her future. But then, I know the routine of the state hospital. One simply cannot respond to all the needs. It is just too overwhelming. One has to become callous or the pain would be intolerable.

I was not prepared to deal with this issue, so I said simply that she had not been discharged. She immediately broke down and sobbed hopelessly and repeated over and over again, "I knew it; I knew it." She was heartbroken.

When I could, I asked her, "What are you fearful of? What do you think this means?" She looked bewildered when I asked, "That you are going to stay here forever?" She covered her face as she continued to cry and shook her head affirmatively. Then I interjected, "Like your relatives?"

Listening requires, at times, verbalizing the heart-cry of another that they cannot speak for themselves. Now she gasped in the midst of convulsive crying, "Yes, exactly."

She wondered how I knew about her relatives. I told her I had taken her history for the hospital—that I interviewed her and also her mother and her brother. I also told her that I was responsible for recommending to the staff that she not be released. I explained that it would be very unwise to have her released now, with a felony charge still pending. "What we need to do is to help you first. Then, at the right time, we will recommend to the court to drop the charges. It is much better if we first ask the court to extend your stay here beyond the ninety days. This already means we think you are sick and thus not responsible for what you did. We also have to make some very crucial decisions first, like where you are going to live. What about your mother? Then, also, what is best for the children? After that, we can talk about discharge."

She then uttered, "Yes, what about the children?" I told her that I was there to plan a visit for her children at the hospital. She was overjoyed with the idea. She spoke freely about how terribly concerned she was for the children since they all saw the horrible incident. When she wondered why we were planning this, I said that I had made this recommendation at her staffing and the superintendent thought it was a wonderful idea. "But why for me?" she blurted out.

"Because your children need to see you so that they know you are all right, and because you need to see the children. After all, it is Christmas."

When she returned with the "Why me?" again; I simply said, "Because we do care for you." Her only reply was, "I guess you must."

She now became deeply concerned about what the children would remember and how they must feel about her. I responded by supporting the deep anguish over the effects on the children, for they might remember very well. It was, after all, only three months ago, and it no doubt made a profound impression. Too, it resulted in the home being broken up and all of them going into foster care. How could they not remember? She was horrified at the thought when I asked, "What will you say if they ask?"

She replied, "I guess all I can tell them is the truth."

"And that is?" I queried.

"That I was just terribly sick. That I couldn't help it."

"And is that very hard to say?" I asked.

She added, "Yes! But I'll do it."

My response was, "The children need you at this time, and to tell them is the right thing to do."

She sighed as she said, "Anything for the children."

I then pushed her even farther, "And if they don't ask, will you take the initiative to tell them?"

Another haunted look, "Must I?" Then a pause, "I guess I have to do that, too."

The subject of gifts for the children came up. I told her about the assistant superintendent's offer to buy gifts. She gulped hard after this. I assured her that the assistant superintendent was herself the mother of a number of small children and knew the meaning of gifts at this time. I also offered to call her family so that if they wanted to give gifts these could also be waiting under the tree for them.

In parting she grabbed my hand in a final, "Thanks so much. How can you?"

A few days before Christmas, the big day was scheduled. I went for Mrs. Smith in the admissions building. She was neatly dressed in clothing that her relatives had brought for the occasion. The ward personnel had cared for the clothes and now had helped her get dressed. A whole crowd of staff and patients accompanied us to the door, with loads of good wishes. "Have a good visit, Joanne." "Kiss your children once for me." "Oh, you are so lucky. I wish my children could come." It was almost impossible to get her out of the building. "People are just wonderful to me. I've never known this before. People in here aren't crazy," she said.

We arrived at the social service building early, so we waited in my office for a moment. She was far too excited to talk. Suddenly we heard the voices of children coming from the parking lot. She ran to the window and shouted, "Oh, there they are. Oh my, how they've grown. My darlings! My darlings!"

I left her in the staff lounge as I went to meet the children and their social worker at the far end of the hall. The three-year-old at the hand of his eleven-year-old brother greeted me with, "Where is my Mommy?" I merely said, "At the far end of the hall, go find her." With that he saw her and ran as fast as he could shouting, "Mommy! Mommy!" I saw him make one leap for her neck as she cuddled him, and then bent down to embrace the other two.

All up and down the hall, office doors of social workers opened to watch, for a moment, and then quickly closed again. I later learned that more than one had became so overwhelmed by the anticipation and the sight of this culmination that they dissolved into tears. A very unprofessional response!

The guest social worker entered my office to synchronize our efforts and also leave the family to celebrate their visit in their own way.

An hour later we joined the group. Mrs. Smith was simply remarkable. She and the older boy sat together, each with an arm around the other. With her free hand she was helping the two younger ones play with their gifts.

We agreed on another hour. It just was not right to end it yet. As we again returned to the visiting room, all the gifts had been packed. They had tasted the lunch, but it was obvious that to have each other was more important to them by far. Mrs. Smith carefully took one child after another and paid attention to each for just a moment. These children meant all the world to her. The extreme attachment of the children to her made parting very difficult. We had to explain over and over again to them: "Mother is still sick. She must stay in the hospital. We will take care of her. Your foster mother will take care of you until you can all go home again." The final leaving was occasioned by many kisses and then waves as long as they could see each other.

I asked Mrs. Smith to sit down with me right where the visit had occurred to review with her what had happened. Her feelings could no longer be kept under control and she let go with a gush of tears. I encouraged her to keep crying. That was the most appropriate thing to do. It took a long time for her to stop. In the midst of it she repeatedly said, "Thank you; thank you." And then she began to talk; a veritable stream of words flowed from her. The beauty of the experience she had just had helped so many things fall into place:

"For the first time in my life, I count; I make a difference; I matter. The smallest thing that bothers me is someone's concern. Everybody understands; the doctor understands; you understand." Then, with intense emotions, she added, "And nobody understood on the outside. I will never be ashamed of having been at a state hospital. The other patients say this has ruined their lives, but not mine!"

"Even my boyfriend is ashamed of my being here. He has been here only once to see me, and yet he hung around my apartment all the time before. He came only for what he could get from me. There will be no more of that. I am finished with him. He isn't even a friend. He didn't care about me. When I was at my worst, all he could say was, 'You ought to be ashamed of yourself.' That's not caring. I couldn't help it; he should have known. He can go where all the rest like him go. I'm finished with him. Why? Why didn't people understand long ago? For years I've been in such desperation, and all I heard was 'You'd better get ahold of yourself.' How could I get a hold of myself? I tried and tried. I couldn't. God only knows how I tried. I told people I was going to pieces. All they could say was, 'They are going to put you away.' Nobody asked me to tell them what was bothering me. Couldn't they see that I couldn't take it?"

I simply added, "It's beginning to make sense, what happened to you, isn't it?"

After this, words rolled out as she talked on and on. She talked about the deprivation of her childhood, in a fatherless home. It was obvious that, with all the children her mother had, she was never wanted. Her mother had depended on community hand-outs; she was the poorest-dressed child in school. Now she was back in the same predicament—penniless—except for welfare funds. And now she had to cope with her mother, whose anger was still very evident. Yet she couldn't leave her mother, because the mother's welfare check made survival possible.

"Why didn't people stop it before it had to get to that horrible episode? For weeks before, I was so totally confused that every day I drove my car aimlessly about the countryside. I had all my children with me. No one even did anything about my boy not showing up at school. I kept saying that I was looking for Joanne. It felt like I had lost myself and I needed to find me. I stopped at many homes, my pastor, my doctor, friends, relatives and neighbors in my childhood community. I kept on asking them if they had lately seen Mrs. Joanne Smith. They didn't know what to make of it. Some had me stay for coffee. Others said, 'You'd better get a hold of yourself, or they will put you away.' Someone suggested a spiritual advisor who I went to. I did anything. Nobody, but nobody, stopped me long enough to find out that I was totally falling apart. No one could see how awful my life was. Then, when my advisor told me that my mother was the devil and I should get rid of her, I thought that I was to kill her. So I did what I thought I had to do.

"I'm so grateful that she is all right. All her wounds are completely healed. But now, I'm not caught. I feel so free inside and you don't know what that means after all those years." Then, a moment later, she added, "Sounds silly to say I'm free when I'm committed to this place."

I replied, "No, it's not silly to me. One can be free at heart even though one's body is in bondage. You were far more imprisoned most of your life than this hospital could ever do."

"Just to think that I should have to go to a state hospital to discover that. In my family here's where you went to die, not to live. To end up in a state hospital meant exactly that. You stayed until your end." Just then she surveyed the room and asked, "Who baked those cookies? They were fresh."

I answered, "My supervisor. She stayed up late last night to do it. She did it especially for you and your children."

"What about this room? Who decorated it?"

I replied, "Well, quite a few people got in on the act, including a number of patients." She couldn't answer because she was all choked up.

After this she looked up at me in a fearful way, as she said, "Do you know that my youngest boy asked me where I kept the ice pick that I used on grandma?"

"Oh my! That must have been a shock. What on earth did you say?"

"And that's not all. He asked if I would ever use it on them, also."

My response was simple shock. She slowly tried to recapture the scene. All three stood near her waiting for her to talk about it. So she simply pulled herself together, put her arms around them, and explained everything. She especially explained that she had no ice pick and she would never again use one. She really loved her mother. Then she repeatedly told them that she had been terribly, terribly sick—that this was why she is now in a hospital. She is still sick and needs more help.

When I asked how they accepted it, she said she thought very well. They seemed to understand as she embraced each one very tightly and told them she loved them, and they seemed to love her doing it.

Then in an almost childlike way she said, "Did I do right?"

I added, "Simply marvelous. It is so good that you could talk about it. This is the beginning of healing the past. I'm sure they heard every word you said, but especially felt the love you showed."

She added, "You know you prepared me for it. I could never have done it alone." She finally sat up as she said, "I know I have a tough journey ahead, but I will make it. I will never again live with my mother. My husband—I must divorce him. He will never be released from prison. I can't live alone and I feel so guilty relating to men, being married. The children are doing so well in foster care. They have such an understanding social worker, and she says their foster parents love them."

I told her that we were going to face all of these problems before she would be released. She still needed our help. This would include a number of visits with the children, finding a new apartment, working out money matters, and advice on handling her relationships with men.

She abruptly turned to me and asked, "Are you going to continue doing this with me?"

I said, "Yes."

"How do you know that?"

"Because I asked to have you assigned to me as long as you need help from us."

"Oh, good," she replied. "I want you to do it. You care so much for me. I even noticed that you got tears in your eyes when I talked about something very sad."

Slowly and silently we walked back, on that cold winter day, to the admissions building. We knew that something profoundly beautiful had happened to each of us.

Somewhere along the way she softly said, "Why, oh why, must someone go to a state hospital to find out that people care? Why can't people on the outside do it? It has been such a long time since anyone knew how much I hurt."

She required no answer.

Just as I inserted the key to unlock her ward, she turned around and suddenly exclaimed, "Jesus is here. I know he is because I can feel him." Then, for a moment, she stopped and said, "Am I crazy?"

"No," I replied. "You're not crazy, Jesus is here. Jesus himself said, 'Where two or three meet in my name, I am with you.' And so, in fact, he is here."

"Oh, that's beautiful. I knew it!" she exclaimed.

In listening with love to Joanne Smith many voices could be heard.

JOANNE: *Listening with Love Is Contagious*

The loudest message that her life was screaming is fright. She felt the severity of her attack on her mother would bring punishment. When I met her, she had already been picked up by police officers, had spent several days in a county prison, had appeared before a judge for a suspended sentence in a state hospital. So what happens to a person like that?

The next voice came from the dread of the future. She assumed that she would spend the rest of her days in this asylum. It had already happened to several of her family members. Considering what she did prior to her admission, how could there be any hope for her? Then, would she lose her children forever?

I could also hear her childhood crying. She had grown up in abject poverty and been abandoned by her father in infancy. Then, in a desperate move to escape all this, she had married far too young to a man who abused her.

The voice of a world crumbling in on her could also be heard. There had been a series of disasters, any one of which could devastate anyone. Her husband had molested her child sexually and she had been forced to have him committed to a state prison, perhaps for life. Soon she was desperate, just as she had been as a child, again under her mother's control. Now, her own children were in poverty and she was taken advantage of by men. All this happened and no one heard her pain.

I also hear a strong person in the midst of all this rubble. Adversity gave her strength to bear the unbearable longer than most people would. If this power to live can once more be released for purposeful living she will make it.

It is valueless to hear all the messages that a life is shouting unless one hears the message to respond. This is where love enters. To be suddenly overwhelmed by the need of this woman and then to act on her behalf is what had to be done. Joanne needed someone to act on her behalf. She needed an advocate. This right was assigned to me. I could do for her what she could not do for herself. After I sorted out all the screaming messages of her life, I knew I had to act, if I cared at all. The most important response was arranging for her and her children to get together at all cost. Healing for all could not occur unless they could see each other, unless the mother could have a chance to explain to the children what had happened in that apartment only a few months ago. Once this was done her life unfolded. A life had been correctly heard.

In dealing with Joanne it is these voices and many more that I had to listen for, in order to respond to her appropriately. Then, when I did, she mobilized all her inner resources to begin life again. Only now she moved ahead with a sense of inner strength and personal certainty that she discovered in a state hospital. All this happened because someone heard the cry of her life and responded with love. It is the power of love that broke the vicious cycle of destruction, despair and defeat.

To really care is to discover life, but one must pay a price. It takes courage to open oneself up to another's pain. It means bearing that pain with the other. And that means hurting just like the other person is hurting. To really care is to take a portion of the other's burden and carry it for him. It can be heavy, just as it is for him. To care is to choose to do it when one doesn't really have to.

One can choose not to hear the suffering of humanity. It only means walking past the hurt man on the side of the road. It is very easily done and no one will know. But one really pays a price for doing it. In the long run, the life of one who refuses to listen becomes less; it shrivels up. The ultimate price of selfishness is puny existence—and that is a living death.

In listening we are made whole. Listening brings into focus the ultimate reason for living. After all, it is for another that one must live, or one doesn't live at all.

Every illness, every injury, every human frailty and need is an invitation to listen. To respond to suffering with care gives life both to the one suffering and to the one who ministers to that need.

We have so many ways to avoid caring. Often we think in terms of handouts, gifts, or things, but there is no heart to go along with it. William Osler, a famous physician, knew what this meant when he said to his medical students, "The only way to care for a patient is to care for the patient."

If we don't listen, caring becomes a technique—a medical technique, a financial technique. This is not really caring. In the midst of all our technology people are deteriorating because things do not satisfy. They need people—people who will meet them where they hurt.

We may become overwhelmed by this assignment. There just aren't enough of us to go around. I have come to terms with this by saying to myself that I am only responsible for the "appropriate others," not for everyone. At one moment it is a client in my office. Then, it is the overwhelmed human being I might chance to sit next to, or the one I see in pain and lean forward to meet. It's not the number, but the condition of the heart that counts.

Amos Fortune knew that caring was contagious. It

was love that set him free from the bondage of slavery. After that he purchased the freedom of others as often as he could. He was now compelled to do for others what had been done for him.

His wife, whom he had first freed, then married, approached him one day and said, "You'd set all the world free if you could, wouldn't you, Amos?"

He shook his head, for he knew that was an unrealistic dream and not for him to do. His answer defines every man's task. "Just the part of it that I can touch. That's all any man can do."*

---

* Elizabeth Yates, *Amos Fortune, Free Man*, (New York: E. P. Dutton & Co. Inc., 1967).

2

MONTFORD
In Which I Listen to Myself

First an angry glare, then, "Why the heck didn't you come in immediately? A wound like that has to be attended to right away. That is an awful mess to clean up now." This was the doctor's response to first seeing the ugly gash across the back of my index finger.

It was late in the day when I arrived without an appointment at his office. There were no patients in the waiting room anymore. A nurse was busy behind the counter shuffling the final papers for the day. There was no doubt that she was tired as she snapped at me, "Do you have an appointment?"

I said I didn't, as I carefully removed the huge fur glove from my right hand. The dried blood made it difficult. One look at the cloth wrapped around my hand brought a shriek, "Oh, for heaven's sake!"

As she was about to call the doctor, he came rushing out of a rear office busily putting on his fur coat, cap, and gloves. It was still thirty below zero out there and obviously he had other concerns on his mind. He appeared not even to notice me, but the nurse stopped him.

"This is an emergency. It has to be taken care of immediately." Grudgingly he came over, took one look, and then the angry exclamation, one I shall never forget even though it has been decades since it happened. "All right!" was his reply as he removed his coat to return to an inner office.

The nurse knew it was up to her to unravel the crude homemade bandage. She carefully soaked it as she unwound it. When she asked what happened, I simply could not respond. How could I ever tell these people? How could they understand? It was such an incredible drama that to give a few hasty details was very wrong. So why talk? They really didn't care. This was an intrusion on their lives. They didn't want to be here; I was forcing them. Audibly I said, "Oh, just a little accident."

The cut extended more than halfway around the back of the finger, exposing the bone. Even as I am now writing the scar is clearly visible, and a deep indescribable feeling vibrates through me as I look at it. However, I must go on because this moment taught me an explicit lesson about life I had really spent years getting ready for. It left an indelible impression that I know is observable to many.

It was routine for the doctor to anesthetize the finger and carefully suture the gash in an even stitch. Finally he asked, "Exactly when did this happen?"

"At five in the afternoon yesterday."

"Then how could you wait until now?" he growled. "How crazy can you be? You look like a sensible person. I don't get it."

I asked him if he really wanted to know. He seemed to think that the situation was so incredible it was worth his time to listen to me. Maybe he even thought that it had been done deliberately and that I was attempting to hide the truth.

MONTFORD: *In Which I Listen to Myself*

"Okay," I remarked. I sensed that he did want to know as he sat back in his chair to hear it in full.

"I am a school teacher in a small one-room schoolhouse in the Montford School District, approximately twenty-five miles away. It is completely isolated with no telephone."

"But," he interrupted, "You look far too young..."

"I am. I am only twenty. I graduated from high school last June. I took eight weeks of Normal School at Moose Jaw, Saskatchewan last summer and I was licensed to teach."

He knew that this program existed so he accepted it.

"Yesterday," I went on, "I was in school as usual. There were twenty students in attendance with all eight grades represented. Around noon a snow storm hit so suddenly that there was no way of leaving the schoolyard. No parent could risk driving their horse and sled across the miles to come for their children. Apprehension filled the classroom. Some of the younger ones began to cry out of fright. I kept soothing them by telling them that the storm might subside, but it was very apparent that it was getting darker and darker as the blizzard got worse and worse. The coal furnace in the basement was stoked to capacity as the room temperature began dropping to below forty degrees and a spray of snow could be felt halfway across the room. I tried to go on teaching, but everyone glanced fearfully at the huge windows every few minutes.

"These children knew how vicious snow storms could get. From early childhood they had been told of casualties and personally knew the terror. By midafternoon it was too dark to read and there was no electricity or any other artificial light.

"At that moment I made a decision. I told them that there was no hope of this storm subsiding. We could stay here no longer. My teacherage—a special house built on the school grounds as for all teachers on the western prairies—would have to accommodate all of us. So we all put on our heavy outer clothes in preparation to leave. My instructions were that we would hold hands in a continuous chain. I would take the lead, the youngest next in line, until the oldest fellow at the end. The teacherage was only fifty feet away from the rear of the school, but, due to the storm, we could not see it. The wind could have been up to seventy or eighty miles an hour. We then proceeded.

"We stayed close to the school building as we moved around to the farthermost corner. I then led the way into the blinding freezing snow, knowing the general vicinity of my house. All went well as I directed."

As I told this story, I knew I had won my audience. The doctor remained silent. He was deeply moved. We were alone since he had dismissed the nurse as soon as he knew he could handle it. So I proceeded.

"The house had only two small livable rooms, plus an unheated room where the fuel was kept. The children expected no comfort. They had endured much already. It was only a matter of delegating responsibilities, and they got busy.

"I first told them that the coal-burning stove was adequate to heat both rooms, that I had ample canned food on hand for supper, and if need be there was space on my bed for all the little ones and space on the floor for the rest.

"Everyone kept their heavy clothes on while I carefully fed the stove to its optimum heat. In an hour they began to settle down. My several kerosene lamps provided sufficient light.

"After this I requested that the older boys take all the younger children into the bedroom to play games with them. Even these had to be imaginary since I owned none. But then, imagination is fertile in such a limited environment.

"The older girls remained with me in the kitchen to make the evening meal. Although they were only in their early teens, they had long ago learned how to make the most out of the least. A menu was quickly worked out, even though it varied due to my limited quantities of food.

"We had no sooner begun when the tragedy occurred. I was opening a tin can with one of those simple can openers. No doubt I was in a hurry. Before I knew it the can took a quick flip and the jagged edge of the lid diced my finger. A circle of girls about the kitchen table gasped as they saw the spray of blood strike a nearby wall. Instantly I covered the wound with my handkerchief and ordered them to keep quiet, not to tell the little ones, and keep on making food.

"I quickly went into the coal room to apply a tourniquet with my handkerchief. When an older girl followed, I asked her to quietly get a clean pillow case from the bedroom and come help me. This we tore into strips as we bandaged the wound. The bleeding could only be stopped with the tourniquet in place. I returned to the kitchen to help, but I left every ten minutes to permit the blood to circulate. Then the bleeding always started again.

"After this the older girls took over everything. The

food was served to everyone, although some had to eat directly off the table, since there were only a few plates. Others used kettle lids, saucers, or whatever could be found. The little silverware was shared. Later they cleaned and washed up everything just as they had to do at home.

"The evening was spent using all the gimmicks we could think of to pass the time, and to keep everyone from getting frightened. We played games, sang, and I even resorted to my knack for fabricating endless stories—an art I, too, learned in my prairie home while the blizzards roared for days on end.

"My finger needed less and less attention. By then I had a large wad of cloth tied around it and there was no need to cut off the flow.

"Bedtime came and we faced the inevitable. We had to spend the night there. The question of whether their parents would know what happened haunted several of them. They feared their parents might have tried to come after them and gotten lost. Or worse yet, perhaps the parents would think they had been dismissed before the storm hit and were freezing to death enroute home.

"I explained to them that I believed the parents knew how suddenly it began and would know that, since I knew all about the prairie storms, in no way would I have taken a chance. I believed the parents trusted me and trusted that we would know how to survive. The children appeared to believe me, because they settled down for the night.

"Five small children got under the covers in my bed. Their outer clothing was used by others for pillows and coverings on the floor. Everything I owned, including my other clothes, sheets, and towels were needed for bedding.

"As for me, I could not take the chance and go to sleep. My finger could start bleeding again. Besides, I had to keep the fire burning at maximum capacity at all times. Such a kitchen stove was dangerous if left unattended with so big a fire.

"It was a long, long night for me. Several children woke up for periods of time so I carried on a whispered conversation to pass the time.

"Morning arrived late at this time of the year. At approximately nine o'clock the first of the sleds began arriving to get the children. The storm had stopped totally. It was bitter cold and everything was covered in a thick, hard, white cover. The parents were grateful, although they had lived through so much that they took it all in stride. Just another one of the endurance tests of life. I believe that they were even grateful that their children had to endure it, since in their minds this was a more valuable lesson to learn than all I could teach in the classroom. Life is cruel and you better beat it or else it will beat you.

"Then how did you get here?" By now he was concerned and really wanted to know.

"Well, one of the families owned a telephone, so I asked them to call Smith Airways, here in the city, to come get me. They did not come until late in the afternoon. The pilot told me he and the other pilots had been in the air all day. Most of these were rescue flights to snow-bound automobiles. Many people had to be hospitalized. So I guess mine was minor compared to the rest.

"Although I must admit that whole day alone in

that little hut was an endurance test all of its own. By then I didn't care if I lost my finger. All I wanted was to get out of there. The Piper Cub on skis coming into view was a beautiful sight. The pilot flew low over the school as I ran out to wave at him. With one wide circle he landed on his skis in the field, then came gliding up right next to my door. I quickly threw all the water out, since everything would freeze solid before I'd get back. Even my tea kettle has been frozen till it burst while sitting on the stove."

The doctor sat speechless for a while. He seemed not to know how to respond. Finally we both got up to go. When I asked for the fee, he replied: "You have paid a bitter price already, there is no fee."

Then, as a parting word, he said, "You are deceptively strong for your age. I guess when you have to endure like you have, it gives you power to do so."

In order to listen effectively to someone else, one must listen with open ears to himself.

As an example I shall now proceed to hear my own message, especially as it was triggered by the previous ordeal with the schoolroom full of kids. In no way is this a composite picture of myself, nor is it necessarily a balanced view. It is only picking up the particular message that I now hear my life speaking to me. Whether it is an accurate or an objective view matters far less than the fact that this is how I see it. How I hear my life is how I experience myself. That is what really counts.

I remember the incident at the Montford school as if it happened only yesterday. There are many other incidents just as vivid. They are not simply amusing episodes. They are the experiences of my past that tell me a lot about myself. To these I must listen very intently and very sensitively so that I can know myself. The more I recall them and cherish them, the more profound messages I hear them speaking about myself.

If I don't listen to myself I cannot hear other people. When I try, without knowing what my life is saying, to tune in to someone else, the message I think I am hearing may not be theirs at all. I may only be hearing the static of my own unresolved past. My past is screaming to be heard and I must listen to it, then sort it out from the stories of other people.

The first message I hear when I listen to myself is that it is suffering that has made me so "deceptively strong," as the doctor said. Several years ago I was eating alone in the University cafeteria. I was deeply preoccupied with the class on Personality Development I had just taught. It had been an extremely emotionally draining experience, although all I had done was to orchestrate twenty-five searching social workers who were attempting to understand personality—their own as well as that of others. Suddenly one of the students from that class appeared from nowhere and briskly asked, "How does it feel to have such power over a room full of graduate students?"

I was startled, but after a moment of thought I said exactly how I felt in one word, "Accountable!"

"Good," she said, "then I am in safe hands," as she rushed away with her empty tray.

Obviously the whole class episode had affected her very deeply and she began to fear whether she could really trust her life into my hands. If only I could have told her that my strength had been tested over and over again in life. Already at twenty years of age a schoolroomful of small children and their parents had trusted my guardianship. And we all survived! For me this was a major claim of my strength.

The deceptive quality of this also needs mentioning. I have been extremely shy and quiet most of my life, and in many situations I will revert back to this again.

As a grade school student I was so self-conscious that I blushed for every offense or at the embarrassment of every other student in the classroom. There were times that I claimed guilt and punishment for things that I didn't do because it was easier to do that than to deny it and try to explain my red face.

I still can feel the fear and trepidation with which I began teaching at the Montford school. It was while I was teaching there that I learned to speak the English language fluently. It was there that I first discovered that I could switch my thought process, while speaking, from Low German to English. Up to that time all the English I spoke was translation and many of my sentences followed the German word order. "Petrified" is the only word that adequately describes my feelings the day the superintendent of the Swift Current School Unit sat listening quietly in the back of the schoolroom. It was no small wonder that my contract was "terminated" at the end of one year.

I now know that I am an acutely sensitive human being. I hear voices and messages long before people begin to speak. Some people in public places will deliberately avoid me because they feel I will see their secrets no matter how hard they try to hide them. Intuitively I hear the cry of a person in pain long before I see his tears. I now claim this art as a gift that helps me find my unique place in the scheme of things. It was at Montford that I was taught this lesson.

MONTFORD: *In Which I Listen to Myself*

The illustration is set in a very cruel world. That is exactly what I was born into. As if to underscore this, even the weather was cruel on the western prairie. Temperatures of more than a hundred degrees, high winds, and dust storms were common in summer. The opposite was true in winter with forty degrees below and snow storms that could bury a community for weeks on end.

Probably the poverty of the rural community was even more vicious. How frequently as children we were told that we had no money! To make the point even more vivid, we were reminded that shortly after my twin and I were born my father drove four miles with his team of horses to the nearest store to get ten-cent pacifiers. His request to charge them was denied because his credit rating was too poor. He was abruptly asked, "When do you think you will amount to enough to pay for them?" Christmas was always a very fearful time because of the possibility that one year we would wake up to no gifts, simply because my parents could not afford any. But they always scrounged so as to at least buy a note book, a pencil, and, if possible, a set of crayons.

If I listen to this part of my past I hear some very clear messages. I believe it can best be said in the words of a hymn I knew, even as a child: "This world is not my home, I'm just a passin' through"—the sense that life as I now know it is not final, but is only a brief struggle in preparation for the real existence that begins at death.

This mortal life cannot be "it." That is impossible. I'm sure that even as I lived at home with six brothers and sisters in a two-room house, while a snow storm raged outside, and saw my mother creating a nourishing meal out of the limited farm produce, I already got comfort out of the words of that song. "It" had to be somewhere else.

If I listen even more carefully to myself I also hear the voice of my ancestors speaking. They are part of me too. As a child of an Anabaptist heritage whose reference book, second only to the Bible, was the *The Martyrs' Mirror*, I knew that those who came before me fared even worse. At the beginning of our history, back in 1525, a group of counterrevolutionaries arose who stood for the absolute separation of church and state, for the right of each person to live by his conscience and to be accountable for that. They chose to take a position of nonparticipation in government and war and also to be rebaptized upon an adult confession of faith. For this they were stigmatized by the then foul word "Anabaptist." For most of them this meant martyrdom, without any resistance.

One could hardly be more other-worldly than that. They chose to so define their commitment in this world and to live by that in such a way that almost certain passage into the next world was waiting for them. When it did happen, they often rejoiced and encouraged others to follow them, even as the kindling was being lit beneath their feet.

Possibly the one word that my people used to define themselves more than any other was "Pilgrims." As the persecution became more severe in central Europe, they began drifting eastward. They gathered in rural Poland. There they prospered as farmers for two hundred years. As soon as their religious freedom was threatened they moved on to Russia. In another hundred years communism began threatening their faith. That meant uprooting their lives once again, and they

MONTFORD: *In Which I Listen to Myself*

were off to the western prairies of the United States and Canada.

Two words described the attitudes of these people toward each other—*kinship* and *care*. During my younger years there were approximately two thousand Low-German-speaking peasants scattered in twenty villages. I had the distinct feeling that they were all part of my extended family. We were all equally poor. The little we had we shared with each other. We were of one kin distinct from the world beyond.

However, no one was excluded from the concern of these people. How well I remember the native Indian family that was snowbound near our village enroute to the Northern Woods. My parents invited them to come live with us. The temperature in the house was far too warm for them, so they all slept on the hay in the barn. As soon as the roads became passable again they moved on. This was the natural response of all the people because suffering might prove their lot next, and then they would need to receive.

"When I see need, I hurt," I hear a still voice within me speaking.

Now I feel pain in people very quickly. I must respond because I have been there myself. My intuitive perception of others is keen, like a very fine tuning fork. With only a slight tap, the voiceless voice of the silent sufferers calls forth a response. They are all my kin. They belong to me just as I belong to others. So I must hear and heal.

The Naskapi Indians knew all about sensitive listening to oneself long before modern psychology taught us how. They believed that each person has an inner companion at the center of his being whom they called the Great Man. With this person he has to be totally honest, for the Great Man already knew everything about them. In consultation with this inner being, by dreams and inner voices, a person understood the meaning of his life and also received directions. Faithfulness to this inner voice was more important than to any outer voice.

I believe I also have a Great Man who speaks to me from within, only I call him God. To understand his message I must listen to all of myself—the voices of my total past as well as of the present. Fortunately, his voice is already in written form in the Bible. Thus my task is to synchronize the written word from another era and the inner voice. This provides the ultimate direction for my existence.

My inner voices go on and on, speaking messages of joy and agony. I must listen to all of them. They can teach me what I need to know in order to hear the rest of humanity.

I am a part of humanity and they are a part of me. That is what I learn from myself.

As my life goes on, I continue to listen as it speaks to me.

3

KATHY
A Child Is Crying and No One Is Listening

Children speak "Childrenese." Haim Ginott says so eloquently in his book, *Between Parent and Child.** Since so many parents no longer know this language, their own children are strangers to them. It is the parents' problem, not the child's. It is parents who now must relearn the language they once spoke, but have long ago disowned. It is the language of experience; the language of emotions.

Parents often forget this language because it brings back very painful memories of their own childhood when they too were pleading to be heard, but no one understood. So, now, instead of even trying to understand their children, they only feel their own pain that they would much sooner forget.

Parents' most familiar response is to scream at their children to stop their begging or whining or whatever. Parents do not know that these are desperate attempts to be heard. They also do not know that it's their own failure to make peace with their own childhood that makes them react so violently.

"Listen, parents! Listen! Your children are crying, pleading for you to hear," is what I am tempted to

---
* (New York: The Macmillan Company, 1965).

yell at those deaf ears. I can't do that. They will also shut me out. They will define me as childish, and that makes my message invalid, just like their children's pleas.

Yet children do, in fact, speak most clearly. They have not yet learned to disguise their message as we urge them to do in the name of "growing up." The problem is that most adults assume that children have very little to say because their thought processes are not yet developed. Their sentences are simple. Let this not deceive you. Within their simple speech styles are the most poignant emotions that man can experience. Their world is filled with enormous overpowering people and animals, real or fantasy. Very little of this is put into words. Most is acted out in play, in mannerisms, and in imaginary imagery. If we can only tune in on this world which is mostly emotions, we can hear deep inner truths that we as adults need to hear. For children are, in fact, closer to the truth than our own peers. Their message is in everything they do, everything they are, and in all their words combined. If only we could see the world from their undisguised eyes, we could meet them and probably meet ourselves also.

One of the saddest stories is when a child's message is not heard, and no one responds to him or her appropriately. Then he or she needs to adopt illegitimate, unnatural, or even devious ways to communicate. Communicate he must, because he cannot bear the message of his world alone. That is the primary task of parenting. A child's total personality emerges out of the interaction between his own overwhelming inner experiences and listening adults. If these words are not heard or are misunderstood due to the absence or the

KATHY: *A Child Is Crying*

deafness of a listener, then the child will become desperate. He may act this out in total withdrawal or resort to whining. He may even create his own fantasy world where imaginary people do understand him the way he needs to be heard. Or there is the child who adopts a "fit," as happened in the real life drama that is the subject of this chapter.

The purpose of presenting this illustration is to show how extreme or devious a child's effort to be heard can go and how easy it is for parents to fail to hear. Then, it illustrates how easily parents who are highly motivated can be retrained. And finally, it will show the dramatic response of this child.

The drama begins very unexpectedly. I had just delivered a speech on marriage counseling at a health care worker's conference, when a rather large person approached me with a very urgent concern. He said he had seen my name on the program, that he had heard about me through church publications, and he now needed to see me. He identified himself as Mr. Wiens, a fellow Mennonite. This startled me since the location was in New York City and he was a hospital administrator. Mennonites are rare in urban settings like this.

The way he asked to talk to me indicated the matter was confidential, so I asked if we might go to a nearby lounge to be alone.

We began rather casually, even though I sensed his impatience to tell me what was bothering him. I asked what had brought a person of his background, which was evidently rural and western prairie, to New York City. Yes, it was true that both he and his wife had come from Nebraska, but they had met at a New York

City hospital, where he had been assigned on a voluntary service assignment. His wife had come to this same hospital for nurse's training. He had begun his duty as an attendant like most of the fellows in the unit. Since he had a college degree he had been quickly promoted to the administrative office. From there he had come to the attention of the hospital administrator, who quickly made him a personal aide. Soon thereafter, with the encouragement of his superior, he had taken the needed academic requirements and supervised practice to be fully certified as a hospital administrator. Then, when the opening occurred at the present hospital he had taken it.

His wife had completed her nurse's training soon after they had begun their courtship. After marriage they had taken directorship of the service unit near the hospital. Here they had remained for a number of years. Actually three children had been born to them during this time. Presently, they lived in a rundown neighborhood near the hospital.

With a great sense of piety, he described their present living arrangements. The house they had purchased was in a slum section in an almost totally black neighborhood. To set an example he had personally remodeled the house inside and out to show how urban people could live if they desired. This was his way of witnessing against urban blight and unwholesome living.

His simplistic explanations bothered me but I said nothing. We must get to his agenda. He then told me his concern.

"We do not know what is wrong with our six-year old Kathy. Now you must first know that Kathy is the third oldest girl and she is followed by two more

KATHY: *A Child Is Crying*

boys. We have five children under ten years of age. Kathy has 'fits' which we cannot handle."

He appeared deeply bewildered as he described what they had come to know as a "fit."

"Well," he went on carefully, "it is this way. It always begins with an incident and then crying follows. This quickly increases in intensity, until she is hysterical. By then she is completely uncontrollable. During the day she will quickly run to the favorite corner where she has a blanket prepared for herself. At night she simply curls up in bed. Then, in this hunched position, she begins to suck her thumb vigorously until the crying subsides. Every night she falls asleep this way. During the day she remains in this position for a half-hour or more, totally silent and motionless. If we pick her up she is limp like a washrag and totally unresponsive. She appears not to hear or feel anything. In about an hour she comes out of it, but then remains aloof and distant for long periods of time. Not only have we been unable to decrease or stop the 'fits,' but they are getting more frequent. They began several years ago and increased until now there are usually several a day. And just to think that she is due to begin kindergarten this fall."

I asked whether there were any specific events that triggered them.

"Oh yes! We know exactly what sets them off. She has always been fearful of bedtime and that is when they first occurred. By now she falls asleep with a 'fit' every night. Then, a fire or police siren will always do it. Where we lived before, we were very close to a fire station. She will never leave the house unless the front door is left open while she is out. If she discovers it closed, she comes screaming into the house and a 'fit' follows, also any incident with her siblings in which they take advantage of her, or whenever she is punished for any misbehavior."

I voiced my shock at the frequency and the excessive degree of deviant behavior which they define as a "fit." He, too, was concerned, but became more alarmed by my intense reaction.

Then, he very abruptly wanted to know if I knew what was wrong. As I heard him describe the child's behavior, my apprehension was rising. It sounded like childhood schizophrenia, even a delayed form of autism, or something extremely serious. The idea of possible institutionalization crossed my mind. But I couldn't say this, since I hadn't seen the child. So I simply said that it sounded very serious to me.

Upon his pushing me further I did give a possible explanation. I told him that there have been studies done recently that show different personalities develop depending on which child it was. He agreed that the oldest was definitely the self-assured, confident leader type. She was aggressive and goal oriented, just as the study stated. The second child also conformed to the norm in that she was a quiet, inner person who could spend a lot of time alone gainfully enjoying herself, and also made many loyal friends. Then, the third was the one that has the most difficult time in life. It is as if the two extreme positions have been taken by the first two children and the third, if born in quick succession, has to find a difficult middle position. This often leads to personality disturbance, thus making the third born the most likely candidate for therapy. This was a desperate move on my part, which appeared to make some sense to him.

I questioned why they had not sought help before.

KATHY: *A Child Is Crying*

To this he made a lengthy explanation. One major factor was that their Christian training had been so totally focused on trusting God for everything and on not turning to human sources for help, that they could not make the move. Secondly, they knew that if their families found out, as they probably would from the children, they would severely reprimand them. It simply wasn't done in their family.

He then went on to tell me about a maiden aunt of his wife who apparently had also had "fits" as a child and was prevented from seeking help for religious reasons. She was now living on the farm of a relative, almost totally isolated and nearly mute. When the subject of Kathy's behavior came up on their visits home, someone would simply cite the case of the aunt and then call it "God's will."

I asked what they were now considering.

"Well, I want to bring her to you. We talked about it before. I even came to hear you because of it. With kindergarten beginning in four months, something has to be done. Besides, you are a Mennonite whom we can trust."

Had he known how shocked I was and how unsure I was of this request, he probably would have fainted. How could I accept a situation like this when problems so severe belong in the best child guidance clinics and such clinics could be found in New York City?

I asked whether they had considered a clinic. He said that they had. They had even located the names of clinics within a reasonable distance, but they simply could not bring themselves to make the call. Aside from the conscience problem, the idea of a clinic seemed so totally foreign to them.

"But you could see me?" I asked.

"We have to," he said, very abruptly. I told him that the distance was approximately ninety miles one way. I stated my fee, but all to no avail. He insisted on coming.

"Look," I began, "I can promise only one thing. I will only commit myself to an evaluation. Then, if it is wrong for me, I will make a referral which I would expect you to carry through. I also could help you in understanding therapy and maybe even coming to terms with your religious question."

He wanted this, although he wished to call his wife to get confirmation. Later in the day he caught my attention again to tell me that his wife was overjoyed, but that they should first take their annual vacation home and delay the session until after that.

I thought this was a clear cop-out, and that I would never hear from them again. But exactly one month later I got a call that they were ready to come. With a lot of misgiving, I scheduled an appointment for July 10. But then, I had promised no more than an evaluation. I asked them to come alone and not to tell the children where they were going.

July 10—First Session

Peter and Agatha Wiens arrived very early for the appointment. Although they had spent almost three hours on the road, they were ready to get to work. Immediately I saw them, in my mind, as a typical rural midwestern Mennonite couple. Mrs. Wiens looked distinctively Mennonite. She wore a colorful homemade cotton dress, a bit longer than the current style. Her hair was "uncut," worn in braids pinned tight to the back of her head, and topped with a small simple hat.

She was petite with a cute oval face and piercing brown eyes which gave me the immediate impression that she could look right through me. But they twinkled, and danced about the room. She was obviously a very alert and highly sensitive person.

Mr. Wiens wore a rather formal suit with a white shirt and dark tie, and black socks and shoes. He was poised and reserved, about six feet tall, and slightly overweight. He blushed easily and looked uncomfortable, which in my mind appeared a little out of keeping with his professional status. He looked to me like a dressed up farmer from the country.

Mrs. Wiens was quick to get to the subject of psychology and theology and how I could reconcile this. I explained that in my thinking the two need not be at odds with each other. Some professionals had to disregard their faith in order to practice psychology, but I saw that as their personal problem, not a necessary one. When I said that I believed God created personality at the same time he created the body, she seemed satisfied and ready to proceed.

Then, together, they retold the story of their daughter. Mrs. Wiens often wiped away tears as she appeared to be in deep agony over what was happening. As a whole they seemed to be in complete agreement on the facts. They took turns to add more parts to the story without any struggle between them. Even when they corrected the other's information there was no sign of any tension. I did notice, though, that they very definitely assumed that she had the submissive role and he the dominant role in the marriage. This, also, caused no stress as I watched them.

Mrs. Wiens was very concerned that Kathy was doomed to follow in the footsteps of her own aunt. I assured her that behavior like this was not hereditary and that it need not be repeated. She seemed desperate for help and assured me they would do anything they could to assist.

I asked them to carefully listen to their own feelings during the next week, especially at times of the "fits" to see if they could detect any correlation.

When I suggested a reduced fee, largely because of doubts about my ability to help and the enormous distance they drove, he responded with a very abrupt "never" and proceeded to write out the check for the full amount.

July 17—Second Session

A week later a very different couple came to my office. Mr. Wiens was much less formal in his attire. Mrs. Wiens looked exhausted and weary. When I warmly asked if the children had been too much for her, she gushed out a description of a horrible week. There was a steady flow of tears.

She repeatedly looked at her husband as she talked, but he very stoicly would not look at her. She was asking for reassurance from him, but he refused.

She now became more and more upset. I affirmed that it was all right to cry—that she had every reason to be upset, but that she needed to tell me exactly how she felt. "Tears are liquid emotions and must be shared," I interjected. This tenderness from me triggered a hysterical crying spell. I repeated my comforting words, while he seemed immobile.

She soon began describing her feelings toward Kathy. She could not tolerate that child's excessive clinging, grasping, whining, and possessive behavior. It drove her

KATHY: *A Child Is Crying*

to utter exhaustion. At times she was so exasperated with the child that she screamed at her to go away. She simply could not take it any more. Kathy woke at six o'clock in the morning and from that moment until late at night there was no rest.

It felt like she was describing a relationship that she experienced like a sticky net that entangled her. The more she tried to escape it, the more enmeshed she became. Then finally, in utter despair, she struck out in anger.

Her husband sat by in utter disbelief. He knew nothing about this. She had felt a deep compulsion not to let him know, for it would confirm her excessive guilt.

"No, Mrs. Wiens," I began, "this is not all your fault. You are not acting alone with this child. Everybody in the household is part of it. Actually it is impossible to pinpoint a fault or to lay blame on anyone. I do not blame you. I only want to understand all that is happening and then we can begin to make changes wherever they are needed."

After this she mopped her face. She began making eye contact with me. The depth of her piercing eyes startled me at first. I felt such a gaze difficult to maintain. Suddenly I noticed a pleading look crossed her face each time I looked away. I finally chose to retain a steady eye contact as long as she expected it. No doubt she was begging me to understand her desperation and accept her behavior. She had no other way of asking for it. Gradually her face relaxed as her eyes lost their desperation. They softened; then she glanced at her husband and about the room. I now knew she had put me to the test to see if I cared enough to see her through this total ordeal and not accuse her, or, worse yet, abandon her.

Mrs. Wiens was now ready to deal with some of the facets of the problem. She knew I would understand. It was not that she was simply a bad mother or wife that caused it all. I was ready to listen to the whole situation.

She continued, "First, I want to mention the place we live. I know we bought the house because we wanted to be an example in a slum neighborhood. I admire how hard Peter worked to remodel it, but I am trapped in it. I know we did it because we wanted to be of Christian service, but I can't take it. It is so hard to keep the children from playing in the neighborhood. Then, when they do, they learn such awful things. I have nothing in common with the women in the neighborhood. Many are on public assistance and separated from their husbands. There is so much need with these people. They need us, and I do enjoy bringing them food when they are sick, but they are just not our 'kind.'

"I spend a lot of time longing for my people, back on the farm in the west. There, I would be able to drop in on my relatives and they could visit me. That was so beautiful!

"It would even be great if we could do like several of our friends do, who live just beyond the suburbs where they have room for their children to play. We now have a garden out there where we raise all our vegetables. Just to go there is such a relief to me and the children.

"That house is a trap for me," she added emphatically.

No sooner had she said this when he stepped in and with finality said, "Then we will move. We can easily sell this house and build a new one out in the country near the other folks."

Mrs. Wiens was now overcome with guilt. "But can we leave these people?"

I then interjected, "Mrs. Wiens, I believe that you have no choice. You have served your time, but now it is too destructive to you and your family. Soon you will need more help than your neighbors."

"Then you think we could go?" she added, attempting to cope with her guilt.

"Let me repeat, you have no choice. You have no choice."

Then Mr. Wiens emphatically remarked, "I had no idea it affected you so much. We are leaving! I have made the decision."

She looked greatly relieved that he made the decision and she appeared to believe him implicitly.

I then told her that since we were on the subject of her concerns she should reveal all of them and let me deal with them one by one.

"Yes," she said, "I know the way I feel about keeping the house clean and neat, and the children quiet when Peter is home. It's really getting on my nerves."

He responded, "What do you mean?"

"Well, I feel like you have carried so much responsibility all day at the office. You have been hassled enough. So I feel obligated to have a clean and peaceful house for you to come home to. I got a lot of satisfaction in seeing you take the newspaper as soon as you arrived home and then go sit down in the living room and read it, but I can't do it anymore."

He exclaimed, "I didn't ask you to do that. I have no right to that. I won't do it anymore. Why didn't you tell me before?"

"I just couldn't because I really believed it was my obligation."

Then he became very gentle as he turned to her and

asked her to honestly level with him about anything else that had been bothering her.

It now became very apparent to me that Mrs. Wiens had defined her submissive role as complete renunciation of all of her needs and complete servitude to her husband.

"All right!" she began, "Would you please put the children to bed at night, especially Kathy? I simply cannot see the 'fit' that she throws every night."

I asked them now if there wasn't anything they could do with Kathy to put her to bed so as to diminish what appears to be simple terror at falling asleep.

"Yes," Peter said, "there is, but I don't know if it's right for me to do. She likes it if I get into bed with her. She then curls up against my stomach and falls asleep in minutes without a 'fit.' "

I asked him to explain to me wherein there could be a problem. He then alluded to the fact that since she was a girl, would it not cause some perversion if he, a male, had her fall asleep next to him.

My instantaneous response was, "Never, not at six years of age. At sixteen, yes, but she is only a child. Could you please do it every night until our next appointment? I would really like to know exactly what is the source of her 'fits' and also what can be done to stop them."

"If you say so, I will do it," he said in a very matter of fact way. There was a very powerful, decisive quality to this man that was very impressive. He was compassionate. He could make changes in his behavior pattern if he only knew what to do. But he had definitely been kept in the dark.

Mrs. Wiens was struggling with a heavy burden of guilt and obligation, all passed on from her good Mennonite background which defined a woman's role simply. She tried to obey and submit until her back was beginning to break. But now she too was ready to alter the pattern. Her simple trust in me was helpful.

"While we are at it," he began, "what else is there?"

Agatha again continued, as if she had the items listed for years and now was the day of leveling.

"Yes, Peter, please take those children with you when you go on your errands at night or on the weekend. That would be such a relief to be free from them once in a while. And also, they would go willingly if you would not continuously force them to stay in the car while you run into stores."

Peter felt a little embarrassment at this moment, for he recognized that this had been very inconsiderate of him. But again he assured her that he would and pushed her for more.

"No, Peter, I don't want any more. Did I not say too much already?" she replied as she reached over to grasp his hand and squeeze it.

He emphatically said, "Whatever it takes I will do. We cannot continue the way we have. I am deeply concerned about Kathy."

They now wondered if I thought I could help Kathy with the "fits." I told them that I was not sure. I really could not say yet. However I would like to come to their house the following Sunday, at which time I would like to see the whole family interacting, and also see Kathy's behavior, in particular. My main reason for going over was that I would prefer to delay, or to avoid, having Kathy defined as the "patient." I would like if she would not know that she was separated from the other children and selected as the troubled child. It might have to be done later, but to do this causes damage that has to be healed, aside from whatever damage had already been incurred. So I requested that they *not* tell the children that a counselor, therapist, or even a marriage counselor was coming. They should simply say that "a Mr. Schmitt who is a friend of ours is coming just to visit."

July 21—Sunday Afternoon

I arrived one-half hour late due to my unfamiliarity with New York City streets and the ninety-mile trip. The house was conspicuously different, beautifully painted, neat, and tidy.

Regardless of our agreement to make the occasion informal, a VIP atmosphere prevailed everywhere. The three oldest girls were spotlessly dressed in homemade outfits, perfectly patterned after their mother's. Their hair was in braids.

Mrs. Wiens soon left the room. The oldest girl brought in a tray of cold drinks. She acted very poised and motherly as she served them. I noticed that she was large for her age and slightly stout, very similar to the father. The second girl resembled her.

Soon Kathy came in carrying a tray of cookies. She came directly toward me. Kathy was a pretty carbon-copy of her mother. The same oval face, the same piercing eyes. She was nimble and active. She kept watching me, making eyes at me, and showing off as she served the cookies. As a result of this she tripped and fell spilling the cookies. I went to her aid in picking up and kidded her by saying it was fortunate that the floor was clean, thus the cookies were still good to eat. She laughed.

Neither of the two boys resembled Kathy. Mrs.

KATHY: *A Child Is Crying*

Wiens picked up Kathy on her lap in a manner that I sensed she wanted to show me something. Kathy immediately began to twist and turn; she even managed to somersault off her lap onto the floor. She returned for more. She looked like a tiny, restless ball of energy who was using the mother for a gym bar. When for a moment all the children had left the room Mrs. Wiens said, "Did you see how she behaved? Whenever I pick her up, this is what she does. You can't get close to that child. She wears you out." Mrs. Wiens suggested that I try holding her since she thought she would likely come to me.

I began a gradual program of getting nearer to Kathy. It involved a walking tour of the house with the oldest girl holding one of my hands and Kathy the other. She showed me her bed and proudly told me, "My daddy goes to bed with me." The oldest girl added, "Because she is scared."

We spent a lot of time alone together as she piece by piece showed me the contents of a doll carriage in which she hoarded all her possessions. I learned that she was a real scavenger who would pick up anything anywhere, and, once added to the collection, an object was off-limits to anyone else. It meant no one dared touch. The other children had accepted that Kathy's carriage was sacred. At first she only showed the items to me before she returned them to the carriage. As I carried on an extensive dialogue about each item, she allowed me to touch and finally to hold them. Gradually I moved her onto my lap as we continued deeply engrossed in her endless tidbits of things. Included in the collection were her own baby clothes, which were obviously very dear. I shifted my attention from the items to her and with that she sank into my lap leaving the items alone. We talked about her dress, the way her hair was combed, her soft skin which I felt. As this went on she curled up in my arms.

By now both parents were watching. The other children were busy all over the house, not concerned with Kathy. I sensed they had labeled her as different and left her to her own devices, while they did their childlike things.

Kathy began a nose rubbing game with me; she laughed freely but still remained in a curled up position. This ended by Kathy locking into an eye contact very similar to her mother's earlier behavior. When I attempted to break it, Kathy grabbed my cheek and held me to the contact. I assured her that I was not going to look away and I didn't. She slowly relaxed in her cocoon that I made with my arms, as her eyes began falling shut. She did not fall asleep. After ten minutes she lay there smiling at me. I had since begun to carry on casual conversation with her parents.

As time came near for me to leave, I told her minute by minute that the time was ending. She appeared to accept it. Mr. Wiens left to get several containers of fruit and vegetables that they had grown in their garden in the country, in good Mennonite style of showing gratitude. As the other children hilariously participated in this procession, suddenly Kathy jumped off my lap to join the fun, but always keeping an eye on me and also bringing me a potato and an apple. She told me they were for me.

In leaving she waved to me and very delightfully yelled, "Good-by" to me over and over.

I was told later that she began weeping as soon as I was gone, calling me "that man." For many weeks she

KATHY: *A Child Is Crying*

repeatedly said, "I love my mommy; I love my daddy; and I love that man." In her prayers, she frequently added on her own, "God bless that man."

I left the house with several immediate impressions. There was an extreme amount of activity and commotion in this household. Five bright, active children so close together can really create a turmoil. Kathy's hyperactivity made the bedlam worse. Mrs. Wiens' need for cleanliness and orderliness was being tested to the uttermost. No wonder Kathy chose the kind of "fit" she did. The only way she could be noticed was by withdrawing. Thus the "fit" was actually a plea for help.

Kathy was the only child that closely resembled the mother. The four other children were heavier, like the father. I wondered if, on a very deep unconscious level, this child did not trigger in this mother her own unmet need for intimacy, and if in a very subtle way the mother had kept a safe distance between her and this child from infancy on. As this child struggled for the mother, the mother fled for safety.

Kathy's ability to absorb another human being was unnerving. To go all the way with her in relationship was frightening. I, for one, did not know if I could terminate my encounter and momentarily I panicked, but as I touched bottom with her she yielded and separated very naturally. I now knew what Mrs. Wiens was afraid of.

My clinical impression was that, although Kathy had been hurt and was being hurt by this family interaction, she had not been damaged. She was very fluid in her use of other people. Nothing had as yet crystallized. If this family had the resources to make a few major changes, I predicted that the course of this child's development could be altered without directly involving Kathy any further. I sensed a tremendously high motivation and an equally high capacity to change. The infinite trust of this couple in me, as the family therapist, settled my treatment model.

During my long trip home I had ample time to think. I felt a deep kinship with that little six-year-old girl. There was no question about the fact that she was hurting. But then she could be reached so easily and so deeply. That made treatment so hopeful.

I soon saw that the greatest need of this household was real genuine intimacy, yet everyone was keeping each other at a cool distance. Mrs. Wiens had a fabulous need for someone to care for her needs, yet she couldn't ask her husband. She was too programmed for submission, and she helped him take his aloof superiority for granted. But she, too, was crying for closeness. Her intense eye contact in the office was ample evidence how desperate she was, but also how ready she was to respond if someone cared to ask her.

As I listened deeply to all the messages I heard from this family, I could hear many voices. Most of them were crying, but Kathy's cry was the loudest. Since she was the most sensitive, she was crying for other family members. She also was experiencing the brunt of it.

"Yes, Kathy! I hear your cry." I even talked to myself as I drove alone. I was becoming tearful as I let myself listen more carefully. "Kathy! The more you clamor for closeness, the more you get pushed away. Obviously you don't know how to ask effectively, but then, at six, why should you know? The only way you know is to grasp, cling, and paw for it, only to frighten your mother. Then she strikes out at you, telling you to go away. She can't stand it, and you think it is you that she is rejecting. Then all you have left to do is to throw a 'fit.'

"It is an intimate union that you need now, not separation. Only in adolescence will you need that. Now you need an almost total feeling of belonging. At times you come across as if you will absorb a person. I felt it for only a moment, but your mother has to struggle with it all day long. She is frightened enough about such an encounter because she greatly doubts her self-worth."

I now knew what needed to be done. Kathy needed a total union with her mother. This had to be of such depth and of such duration that she would know she really belonged. Then she would arrive at a healthy self-esteem. After this she would let go and have normal relationships that would have deep, wholesome intimacies, as well as appropriate separations.

Kathy's "fits" were all related to separations or threats of separation. To be caught outside on the sidewalk with the door closed caused a panic because it too vividly reminded her of the closed doors between her and her mother and her siblings. The rejection by her brothers and sisters was all experienced as abandonment and thus a cause for a "fit." The same held true for parental discipline. Even going to sleep required a high degree of trust that one belongs, in order to yield to a venture into the dark unknown. Those "fits" all began to make sense.

"You can't wean a child when you have never breast-fed her. You can't push her away from you if you have never met her. You can't say 'go' when you have never said 'come,' " I felt like screaming at this couple, although I was many miles away by now.

I also knew that I could not refer this family. Kathy didn't need to be sorted out from this family and defined as "the sick child," then treated at a child guidance clinic. She was not sick. She was only crying for her mother—the one she never had. She was crying on behalf of her whole family. She was the only voice that this family had. I had heard her that day, so now I had to respond appropriately.

JULY 24—THIRD SESSION

The couple arrived at my office for their next appointment prim, proper, and poised, yet I sensed a much greater level of trust. They definitely felt good about my visit.

I immediately told them that I had concluded that I wanted to continue therapy following our model, and not to personally involve Kathy at all. The fact that Kathy responded to me the way she did convinced me that she was very receptive to help, but that this would have to come through them.

Mrs. Wiens spoke at length about how amazed she was at Kathy's behavior. She said that she had never gone to strangers, even to their own relatives. Then, the way she curled up on my lap simply overwhelmed her. This, to her memory, she had never done, even for them. Her behavior with them was exemplified by her somersaulting.

Mrs. Wiens added, "I watched you very carefully and saw you slowly winning her confidence, until she surrendered totally to you."

KATHY: *A Child Is Crying*

I assured her that I was experimenting with Kathy's ability to yield to a relationship, and my conclusion was that she needed it desperately right then and with her mother.

Next, they wanted to know on what premise I felt this had any relationship to the "fits."

I now illustrated a model for child development. It was that all people need intimacy to discover their self-worth. Then, after that is fully discovered for that age, they need an experience of separation to discover their individuality.

As I described this developmental process, I made a large zigzag diagram on a tablet. Next, I showed them that there are specific stages in a child's growth when the one need is much stronger than the other. Immediately after birth, a newborn infant needs total union. This is best dramatized by the breast-feeding experience when the infant doesn't even sense the boundaries between herself and the mother. Then, at about two to three years of age, she has her first urge to strike out on her own. That is why this stage is often referred to as the terrible twos. It is an attempt to find out what her body will do for her on her own. Yet, psychologically, she is really making a trial run to define her separate individuality. It is a rather short-lived period. Then, for the next ten years, a child remains close to parents, spending much of the time learning family behavior by identifying with the parents. Teenage is the huge trip away from the family when a child discovers her identity for life. The needed closeness now comes from peers. The childhood development comes to an end as she finds a mate within the peer group with whom she then unites in marriage. At this point she is free psychologically to join her parents and adult friends.

As I completed drawing the diagram with all the notations on it, Mrs. Wiens asked, "May I have that diagram? I will need that to remind me."

I asked, "To remind you of what?"

"That there are two different needs, both intimacy and individuation; that the one is being met by closeness and the other by letting go."

I then asked her if she knew what Kathy was screaming for. "Oh, yes, I do very, very well," was her emphatic response. "I know what she needs, but I have two problems: One—can I give her what she needs? And two—if I enter into such a relationship with her, will she ever let go?"

My answer to the first was that we simply have to experiment with one week at a time, with my giving her all the support I can and her husband doing the remainder.

Internally I breathed a sigh, "Parents can learn to listen to their children with love, if they are helped to do so."

To the second question, I said that I was confident that Kathy would let go because I had seen it many times before and, also, this was according to the book. If a child's need for closeness is met to the depth of that need, then the child terminates it on her own.

Then came an instantaneous emphatic response from her, "Promise?"

I was momentarily startled, but she continued, "You know how clinging that child can be. I feel like she wants to eat me up, and there is no end to it."

I deeply identified with her. It was a chance she must take. And it wouldn't be easy since she also had very deep needs to belong.

At this moment Mr. Wiens moved his chair closer

to hers as he put his arm around her. "Agatha, I will do all I can to make it possible for you to do this. If need be, I will take my vacation time to stay home. I can leave late and arrive home early since I am really my own boss."

I then asked Agatha how she felt about it and if she saw any way of implementing it.

"Yes," she said, "I already know where to start. Kathy wakes at six in the morning as soon as she hears me get up. My reason for arising is to get as much work done as possible before the children wake. But in no way will Kathy sleep. I have been thoroughly annoyed by this. I have made her stay in bed. If she does get up, I make her keep quiet as I work. I now know that this is when she is the most in need of me. I believe if I offered to hold her she would respond to me like she did to you on Sunday."

I then interjected, "Could she maybe be getting up to have you for herself before the other children wake and compete for you?"

"Oh, yes, very likely. She seems pleased to be near even if she is forbidden to talk. O.K. I know what to do. Beginning tomorrow morning I will do with her exactly what she wants. And that, I believe, is to sit in the rocking chair holding her while I rock her and talk with her."

"Good enough!" I responded. "That is an exact starting point, and I suggest that if you are able to endure it you hold her until she gets off. May I ask further that you pick her up whenever she comes to you at any time all day? Drop anything you are doing and respond to her."

"That is asking an awful lot, but I will do it," she replied with determination.

"Oh, by the way," came the final remark from Mr. Wiens as they were leaving. "I have crawled into bed with Kathy every night. This has ended the 'fit' at bedtime totally. She falls asleep within minutes. Then I leave."

I bid them adieu as I invited her to call if she became overwhelmed by the request.

August 1—Fourth Session

At the next session the couple came in looking strained, although determined to continue. The extent of Kathy's need for closeness had come as a shock to all of us. For the first several days she had seemed hardly able to let go at all. The morning ceremony lasted for hours. Even during the day she would frequently say, "Hold me Mommy," and then would curl up on her lap and feign sleep. In between these sessions she was hilarious, skipping around and saying over and over again, "I love my Mommy! I love my Mommy!" then dash to her for another session.

With the other children Mrs. Wiens had made the agreement that they were not to say anything about what she and Kathy were doing. Since they were so familiar with her "fits" and also used to that word, she had told them that this was to help her stop them.

There had been no "fit" during the first week. We were all encouraged that we were on the right track, even though no end or let up of her possessiveness was in sight.

Mrs. Wiens derived a lot of strength from her relationship with me. She often smiled very warmly to me but always with the expectation that I would return it. The eye-locking game was repeated several times in

KATHY: *A Child Is Crying*

this session and it continued intermittently as long as I knew her.

It helped Mrs. Wiens to be so sure of her husband's support, which he proved beyond question.

My repeated defining of the sucking, clinging quality of Kathy's need helped them to understand the whole process. Mrs. Wiens always brought the chart I had drawn along and often kept it on her lap to help articulate where we were in this whole process.

August 7—Fifth Session

Mrs. Wiens had arrived at the end of her endurance. She was totally exhausted. Even the neat hairdo and the meticulous clothes were absent. She had been crying when she arrived and cried through much of the session. Often during the week she had said to herself that this was the price she had to pay for what had gone wrong between Kathy and herself. She even recalled that many months ago she had told herself that a day of reckoning would come, and this must be it.

She had found it very, very difficult to respond positively that week. She had been tired to begin with, and Peter, too, had been more hassled on the job. As if Kathy sensed this, she had reacted by becoming more possessive than ever. This had resulted in her coming more and more frequently and then staying longer.

I responded by assuring them that I understood how discouraging this must be, and even wondered if she had the strength to see it through to the end.

Then she said that there were two items that had hounded her all week which may have contributed to her lack of patience.

The first had to do with her feelings when Kathy

was born and during her early years as an infant. Again her husband knew nothing of it, but she wanted to tell him in my presence.

She had not been at all ready to be pregnant a third time in such quick succession, especially since Peter was still in hospital administration training. At the time they had two very tiny children, a limited amount of money, and a cramped living arrangement in the voluntary service unit house. Aside from this, she had wanted to continue her nursing practice while they were near that hospital.

Her Christian ethics had been really strained on this issue. According to her background she should have been rejoicing that she was honored to be a mother again. Yet anger and discouragement had overwhelmed her frequently. Her piety had not let her share this with her husband. As a result she had often feared that this child's behavior was punishment for the way she had felt during pregnancy.

I assured her that it could not be punishment since God simply does not behave that way. But the fact that she was not ready for another child naturally would bring negative feelings, and no doubt this was some of the source of Kathy's behavior. Also, Peter was as much responsible as she was for the timing. My reaction to her was that I was really grieved to hear how isolated she must have felt since she kept all this to her self.

"In that case I want to go on," she continued. "You know that I did continue private duty nursing at night throughout Kathy's first year of life. I would put the children to bed, then one of the student nurses would come over and care for Kathy. When she awoke at night and in the morning Kathy often appeared to be very resistive to these girls. Frequently she awoke to total strangers. I knew this wasn't right, but I just couldn't tolerate staying with her and neglecting my career. You don't know how bad I have felt about it over the years." She again became very tearful.

My response was to simply say that obviously herein lay much of the problem at bedtime with the question of who she really belongs to. It was good for Agatha to share it now. It also helped us understand that the course for helping Kathy was correct.

Then Agatha went into convulsive crying. I knew there was more that she needed to say today. With some encouragement she finally began:

"Now I must tell you the worst part of everything. Last summer when we had a family reunion back home, I wanted so badly to visit with all my relatives. I had missed them so terribly much since I hadn't seen them for so long. I was unable to talk because Kathy was clinging and whining continuously. The men were all far away playing ball. The women were together in the picnic grove visiting. Suddenly something came over me as I hit Kathy on the head so she fell to the ground. One of her worst 'fits' followed, and all my relatives looked on with horror. I'm sure they thought I was a horrible mother." All of this could hardly be told in the midst of tears, nose blowing and choking up.

Again, as always, my position was that she is human, with human endurance, and under those conditions it is perfectly understandable that she was pushed beyond the breaking point. I wondered if these thoughts bothered her this week and thus made endurance so limited.

She said that this was the cause, since she feared that I would reject her if she told me. Yet she couldn't see how she could not tell me.

I assured her that as far as I was concerned nothing had changed, except that I understood her better. I now knew the burden she had carried. It was beyond what ought to be asked of any human being.

When I asked her if she was ready to continue the program for another week, she assured us that, now that this was all out of the way, she was sure that she could. She stated that the tenderness of her husband was far beyond her imagination. He thanked her and assured her that he would go all the way.

August 14—Sixth Session

Today some of the earlier radiance began showing through. Her first comment was: "I believe we hit bottom last week and now we are on our way up. There has not been a single 'fit' since the program began. Kathy always wants her morning ceremony, but sometimes it is relatively short. The frequency of her daytime sessions is also definitely diminishing."

August 21—Seventh Session

Everything was improving in every way. The mother had already walked to school with Kathy several times to see the playground. They had met the kindergarten teacher who was young and enthusiastic. Mrs. Wiens had arranged a private session with the teacher to explain Kathy's problem and also the type of help they are getting for her. The teacher had appeared very ready to cooperate.

August 28—Eighth Session

In every way things were better. Both Peter and Agatha looked so relaxed. They were talkative and

KATHY: *A Child Is Crying*

cheerful. They knew they had succeeded. The only apprehension that remained was the beginning of kindergarten the next week.

SEPTEMBER 3—NINTH SESSION

The Wiens couple came in to report progress and to get the little support they yet needed.

They had noticed one change. Lately Kathy had been leaving the house on her own to ride her tricycle. Apparently without thinking about it, she would close the door behind her. She had even ridden her tricycle as far as a block away from home.

The night before school started the mother had been canning peaches and the older children had begged to help. This had been granted under the condition that they would wash their hands properly before they began. The older two had obeyed quickly and returned to claim the best tasks. Kathy had stood motionless; she had appeared confused. Then she had begun crying and fled to the "fit" corner. The mother had known instantly what to do. Calling her husband to take over the canning, she had picked up Kathy and gone to the bedroom to be alone with her. Kathy had responded immediately and pulled herself together. They had then realized Kathy was very aware that school began for her the next day and that they should not have begun the peach canning. The confusion had been too much for her. Then the final rejection had come when she could not compete with her older siblings.

The next day the mother had walked with Kathy for the two blocks to school while Kathy wept. But the mother had accepted it. Fortunately, as soon as the teacher had seen her, she had picked her up and carried her into the classroom, instead of leaving her to wait in line. On each succeeding morning a few tears had been shed on the way to school, but as soon as Kathy had seen the other children she had run off to play. She always arrived home excited about school.

September 10—Our Final Session

We simply rejoiced and reminisced about our three-month journey together. What was most apparent was that Kathy very accurately felt deeply rejected and unwanted. This was the source of her crying. Her "fits" were her only way of screaming for help. She needed to know that she belonged, totally, to her mother.

This couple had been ready to pay the bitter price of getting the message through to her to the full degree of her need. Once she was convinced and her need was met to the depth of her hurt, she could let go.

We affirmed the beauty of this moment worshiping together, for surely God had led all of us. There was no doubt that his love had made all this possible and all of us able to do our parts.

A month later I received a telephone call from Mr. Wiens to share with me their delight in Kathy's behavior. He was apologetic for calling; he was not sure this was permissible, but he said that he could not help but tell me.

The most rewarding change had come a week ago when Kathy had asked him not to go to bed with her. She had said now she was a school girl she was too big to have someone sleep with her. He thought it rather cute of her to ask him if it was all right with him also, since she thought he enjoyed it and would miss it. He had assured her that it would be all right with him and then terminated it.

There had not been any "fits" of the kind that there used to be, although she would cry like any other child at times.

The tears prior to school were intermittent. The mother had also phased out the earlier practice of walking her to school. Mrs. Wiens had discovered that if she spent a brief period alone with Kathy the first thing in the morning it made leaving for school easier and diminished her fears.

In December I received this letter from Mrs. Wiens:

Dear Dr. Schmitt,

Just thought you might be interested in hearing a bit about how Kathy is doing.

There has been constant progress with only a few regressions to the old self. And those are only momentary. School had been in progress a month when we got a notice from the school and Kathy's teacher felt she was able to work better with a more mature group and she was switched to a morning section with the same teacher. She had been in a "slow" section and was moved to the "average." Several weeks after the change, I spoke with her teacher and she gave an encouraging report. She said she's quite shy and quiet but occasionally is volunteering to be used. She said once she was surprised but pleased to have Kathy agree to sing a solo in front of the class. Kathy told me all about it when she came home that day. She was all aglow.

Until about a month ago, she always worried about something before leaving for school. Either she was afraid her best friend wouldn't be at school that day or that she'd spill her milk (it happened twice), or that I wouldn't be home when she came home (that never happened). But I seldom hear her worry about those things any more.

She never requests my husband or I to sleep with her any more. She still worries about hearing fire sirens at night and every night before she goes to sleep she says, "If the sirens wake me, I'll come over to your room and you'll come back to bed with me. Right?" I assure her that she's right and she's satisfied. But she never wakes up when the sirens go. When her class visited the fire house, she came home all excited and kept saying, "And I didn't even cry."

She no longer requests me to hold her every few minutes as she used to. I find it so much easier to give her my complete attention and love when they are further spaced. We do have some moments of contact but I believe these are becoming further apart than even a month ago. She just doesn't seem to need it as often.

My husband and I feel we have made progress too because of our interviews and will always be thankful to you for your help and counsel.

Hope you have a peaceful, meaningful Christmas.

Sincerely yours,
Mrs. Wiens

A year later I met Mr. Wiens at a Health and Welfare Conference. He was really anxious to report further development.

He has accepted a comparable hospital position in Nebraska. They have already purchased a lot in the country, not far from their relatives, and a new house is under construction. He said he now knows that they can no longer stay in an urban setting. The stress is too much for his wife and the family needs to be included by their kin. So they will be leaving the area in a few months.

Kathy is developing normally. She is proving to be an exceptionally bright and very talented child. There is no doubt that she is far more active than the rest of the children, but this is no longer an annoyance to anyone.

He said that he and his wife often talk about the whole experience and have a deep sense of warmth about the entire venture.

It is now very obvious that Kathy was crying and that no one heard her. No one understood what she was saying. But then, how could one expect a six-year old to speak a message that was even beyond her parents' ability to articulate.

The most vivid message of children can be the voice of the entire family rather than theirs alone. Kathy is a perfect illustration. This family was not close. Many deep feelings existed that were never faced and this caused an air of aloofness. Kathy needed to be unconditionally loved and deeply possessed. This can only be done when there is an openness with feelings. She could not tolerate this interpersonal distance and she acted out the pain, not only for herself, but for everyone else. First, the parents closed the gap between themselves. Then, when they included Kathy, the "fits" ceased.

Children speak in symbols. To hear them is to decode these symbols into plain language, and then respond. Kathy spoke by clinging to her mother. When this was not heard, she resorted to more extreme measures. I have just begun to see a ten-year old boy who has severe stomach cramps. Since no medical measures helped, the parents turned to psychological care. It is rather obvious that these cramps are only symbolic of the unresolved cramps that the family is suffering. They have as yet not faced up to this fact. It is my task to slowly include other members and then interpret the message I hear to all of them. The boy's pain is the most audible voice to be heard in this family.

To understand children one must understand the whole family. They are the products of the total interpersonal interaction in the household. To stop and look at the whole family situation helps understand each member. One must take into account the number of family members, their birth order, the exact climate that the entire setting creates. And, even more precisely, one must sense how each member experiences the whole situation. At times of crisis or severe stress, alarms can be heard which can then be used to hear the voice of the family and the voice of each particular child.

Listening with love is the key to relating to all children. They each have their story to tell and it can be heard. If we can dare to learn their language, we will understand it. To hear their voices accurately is an absolute prerequisite to responding to them. Listening and responding with love to children is the art we need to learn in order to create a climate for healthy emotional growth.

4

JIM and LINDA
*The Cry of Adolescents
in the Identity Crisis*

"My problem is that I cannot make a commitment. There is nothing I want to do. If I did want to do it, it means that tomorrow I will have to live with that choice; and I can't tell if I will want it then. Looking at my past, I already know it is likely I will not want it. I have often accepted assignments, appointments, or even dates, and then simply not showed up for them. I feel like nothing is worth making a commitment to. So I do only what feels right now, and with the least consequences for tomorrow."

"How, then, did you get to my office today, when you called to make the appointment more than a week ago?" I asked.

"Well, that's the chance you took," he continued. "Immediately after I made it I told myself that I likely wouldn't keep it. Yet, other days when I really, really got confused, I got comfort out of the fact that I had made enough of a commitment to make it. At least I knew you had a spot reserved for me.

"How can I decide to go to college, because I do not know how I will feel when it's time to go, or when I get there?

"I see myself as a wandering prophet who has caught a great idea—like I need to find the ultimate synthesis of all existence to which I must be faithful. Until I find this idea, I cannot make a commitment to anything. But, then again, I am very sure this is a grand cop-out so that my aimlessness sounds meaningful."

I told him, "I hear a very lonely person crying in the wilderness and no one is really listening." For a moment, I thought he would respond to me, for a deep sense of pain crossed his face, but then he gave this account.

"Immediately after graduating from high school last spring I bought this old panel truck and I left. I was going to find myself before I returned home, so I headed west. Somewhere in the Rockies I met a group of mountain climbers getting ready to make a climb. They were fellows about my age, but really into what they were up to. When I asked to join them they were perfectly agreeable. All I had to do was my share of the work.

"After several days of climbing I fell several times and even delayed the entire expedition. I was badly bruised. The fellows kept telling me what to do. They talked about letting go, told me to stop being so uptight, to get out of contact with the material world and into contact with nature. They said it was not a matter of training for a skill, but of yielding to the mountain. They even were very philosophical about it, for they said that a true mountain climber actually surrendered to existence. But I couldn't do it. I kept on making stupid mistakes. One night they all sat down with me to inform me that I could not go up any higher with them unless I changed my whole attitude. From there on it was very dangerous and they couldn't take the chance. So I told them I would return to the original camp. They even helped me get there, but I was a total failure. I drifted for several more months, westward to the coast. It was all empty, so I returned home."

I wondered if that was where he got the thought of the "great idea" that would synthesize everything.

"Yeh, I guess. I never thought of it before." Then he remained silent. It was as if my beginning to find some explanation for his sense of futility was too much to bear. He could only respond with silence. Total confusion described him best. That he wasn't ready to be rescued was what I heard.

Suddenly a blast of anger erupted. "I hate college. It only warps and bends people's minds out of shape. Professors who are already bent out of shape by their training do the same to others. Most of my buddies are in college, but they are being destroyed by education. I stopped to see several of them on my journey and they are 'goners.' No one is going to do that to me."

I knew he was including me in this category, for he knew I had taught in a university. He was definitely fighting me, too. I might show him the light before he was ready for it. So he struck out in anger.

Then a frightened look crossed his face. "You know I should be in great shape. Dad gives me the money I need. I have a panel truck, which will take me anywhere. Only, I have no place to go. Anywhere on this continent—but where? I don't even know which direction to turn when I walk out of here."

I again reiterated his desperation. Perhaps he needed to trust me enough to hold on to him, while he continued groping in the dark. Then, when he finally would see the daylight, he would know what to take a hold of.

Again he remained silent. Suddenly he sat up.
"Do you believe in God?"
"Yes, I do, but why do you ask?"
"How about Jesus Christ, and the Bible?"
"Again the answer is 'yes'; but what's the problem? Do you, by chance, think that you ought to look there for a commitment?" I asked.

For a while he stared into space, as if in a deep trance. I didn't want to disturb his thoughts.

Then he threw himself back and exclaimed: "That is exactly what I thought. You are just like my parents. Church is everything to them. They are old and never understood me!"

"I'm sorry to hear that this has happened to you. Could you tell me about it?" I inquired.

"Oh, never mind. It's not important. But there is something I do want to talk about. There was this beautiful girl I met in high school. She was so extremely nice to me. When we were together we really got into it—so intense, so neat. But she also was a Christian. I couldn't stand her deep commitment. It meant so much to her, but I couldn't swallow it. I needed someone to drift with me, but she couldn't. She knew where she stood and that frightened me.

"She wanted a future, and I couldn't give it to her. I don't know what the future is, I told her, so how could I give it to her? I don't have one myself. So how could I promise her anything? I couldn't say I loved her, because even that is a promise. This kept up year after year until someone else came along who could promise it to her. Shortly before graduation she turned a cold shoulder on me. She had waited long enough.

"Before, I could always turn to her to fill my void. I know I filled a void in her also, but that was not enough.

JIM and LINDA: *The Cry of Adolescents*

I called her a few weeks ago, from another state, and there was nothing there—even a void between us. She seemed only to wait for me to hang up. That was all. Yet this is the same girl that wanted me so desperately for so long. She even wanted to be married to me, but I couldn't."

Even when I attempted to show that I tried to understand, he appeared annoyed. By now an hour and a half had passed and another client was waiting. When I suggested terminating, due to my schedule, he simply sat staring into space.

"A lost child who happened to stray into a police station, too frightened to cry, too confused to ask directions," I moaned to myself.

As he finally got up to leave, I got the distinct impression that whatever he had come for he had not found. He was disappointed and even more lonely than when he came. The last chance, the last person, and nothing.

What was supposed to happen? I, too, was lost for an idea.

When I suggested another appointment, he remarked, "I likely wouldn't keep it, so why bother?"

As he walked out the door, I said in desperation, "Promise to call me in a week or two."

Back came an answer true to his form. "I don't make promises. Don't you know that?" And he vanished.

My heart aches for you, Jim, as I hear your truck slowly leave and fade away down the street.

If I could only talk to you or your parents and tell you that you are in the midst of a severe adolescent identity crisis. This is the time of your life when you should take all of your past experiences and resources and, with an eye on the future, you should mold and shape your person into who you need to be. You ought to establish a lifestyle that is congruent with all that has been, and what you now are, and then become what you hope for yourself.

But Jim, at nineteen you are not able to do it. I hear your desperate struggle, but you cannot let me in. Your inner resources are depleted. Your world is a void and you cannot face the future. So you drift.

Your identity crisis will end when you are ready to make a commitment to some person and some way of life that is right for you. You faintly heard that voice in the words of your girlfriend. She was bidding you into intimacy and to purposeful life. But, when it came time to choose, you couldn't do it. You simply wilted. That is no choice at all. Then she chose and this left you floundering even more.

As I silently listened to you, Jim, I heard many messages that you could not let yourself hear. I heard the fact that you have always been a very lonely boy. As the youngest child in a large family, your parents were too old, sickly, and tired to respond to you when you needed them. They hardly knew you existed. In the pre-teen period they should have been close to you so you could have sunk in solid roots. But no one was available. Then, when the storms of adolescence hit, you had no mooring. By now they did not know where you were physically and least of all emotionally. Instead of providing you with some boundaries of behavior, they paid off their debt to you with money, only to give you even more freedom which you now could buy. This, you could not handle. When the last structure that high school provided was gone, you were lost at sea without a compass.

JIM and LINDA: *The Cry of Adolescents*

Jim, I know your deepest need is to be separated from adults as you wage your war with yourself in search of your identity. This is why you found it so hard to let me come close to you. If you could complete that search and find yourself, then you could come back and you would be able to be touched. But not until then.

Let us now leave Jim and, by way of contrast, listen to Linda, who is also in the same stage of life. But she is much more successful. She has loaned me her journal and letters to be used to illustrate the identity struggle. Linda is eighteen years old and in college, far away from home throughout this stage of life.

Linda, you are a typical adolescent. Your emotions and your behavior are unpredictable and extreme. At times you are so inconsistent and in severe conflict with yourself. To try to understand you logically is impossible, but when I listen to your feelings, you do make sense.

Teenage is a period of extremely deep emotions. That you already know, Linda. Feelings are the deepest they have ever been or even ever will be again. Your task is to experience all these feelings. Then, as you encompass all of them, you synthesize your identity. You finally have experienced all of these feelings to the extreme that you need to and, since you claim them as your own, your identity trip is over. You will have the sensation that your life is jelling. At that point you are ready to make a commitment, for you then know who and what you are committing.

I once heard a famous psychiatrist describe adolescence in essentially the following manner.

The degree to which an adolescent can venture into

extreme emotions is so great that at any one point he can look psychotic. If an adult would do what the adolescent does, we would diagnose him as sick. But not the adolescent. He is perfectly capable of experiencing these extreme feelings, in any one direction, and with ease can come back from that journey and be ready to venture into another direction immediately. At one moment he is fighting his impulses and is totally ashamed of showing any of them; at the next he can abandon himself completely to them. He may briefly want to be deeply intimate with his parents, yet with one turn of events he can attack them and leave them in utter despair. The teenager is more idealistic, more outgoing, more gracious, than he has ever been before, and at the same time he can be the exact opposite: selfish, arrogant, vindictive, and destructive.

All that this adds up to is nothing more than that it is extremely difficult to discover one's identity. To move from the point of seeing oneself only as an extension of the family to the place where one claims his own separate individuality is an enormously big emotional experience. It is one of the biggest emotional upheavals of a lifetime. But once it is finished, he is finished. He can settle down and live with the size and shape of the self that he was discovered.

Linda, your journal illustrates these emotional highs and lows:

I feel really crummy!!! I think it's partially due to the rain, but not wholly. My former boyfriend is out with my roommate, and that depresses me. It shouldn't; I have no claim on him. None whatsoever. I hope he doesn't ask her out again or I may soon resent her. I can't let that happen! It's hard enough to room with her, and if I resent her that will really cause trouble. She is sensitive, too, and will be able to tell if something is wrong.... When she asked me if I minded her going out with him I said no and meant it. Now I don't know how I feel. At least I have some comfort in the fact that I have a date Friday night.

I wish Dave were around to talk to. I know I depend too much on him, but he's so easy to depend on. I like talking to him: he listens. I mean really listens. It would be so easy to let our relationship turn into something more. In fact it is already. He's so special, but I don't want to "go" with anyone. Not yet, it's too soon.

I wish Dave would call, but I know he won't. I've talked to him the past several nights and I know he doesn't want to make a habit of being with me or talking to me all the time. People will start to say we are "going together" and we're not. He wrote me a letter today and that made me feel good. I should be satisfied with that, but I'm not. I always want more than I have. I have to learn to make myself happy with what I've got.

Next day—

It's funny, I feel so opposite from the way I felt last night. I've been talking to Dave for the past two hours, but I'm not sure I could say exactly what we talked about. I know I was depressed when he called and I was still depressed when he came over.

All today I felt just like yesterday only I was mad at myself for wanting Dave.... I wrote him last night and told him all the things I wrote in here. It's nice not to have to hide anything from someone, to have him know everything you're feeling! We talked about the *fact that I feel funny being so aggressive. If I want to talk I will usually call him, except like last night when I'm mad for being like that. If I want to show him that he's special I feel free enough to give him a kiss. Sometimes I feel like I shouldn't be that way. Girls aren't supposed to be that way. They are supposed to sit back and let the guy make all the "moves." Well, I'm not like that . . .*

Dave is so neat! He just accepts me for the way I am. No strings attached. I really like that.

Later—

Most of today was really crappy. . . . I was disappointed because Dave hadn't answered my letter, but yet I had no right to expect him to. He didn't call, but why should he? Tonight was the same way. I wanted to talk with him, but I wasn't going to do the calling. I was glad when he called but it wasn't enough to get me undepressed. I'm glad he got to see me in that kind of mood. At least he knows a little bit about another side of me. I have so many different sides it would take years to know them all. I'm thinking and feeling so much I could fill pages just from one day, but it's so late and I have class early tomorrow. And anyway tomorrow is another day and I have a date.

Later—

I wanted and needed reassurance and got none. I feel like playing really cool, just letting it all up to him. If he doesn't like me for the way I am, like I thought he did, I don't want anything to do with him and I mean it. I wish I could say "drop dead" and mean it.

JIM and LINDA: *The Cry of Adolescents*

Why?
How do I get myself into these messes?
Today has been such a bad day. I dropped my tray at lunch. I didn't talk to Dave, even though he was in the cafeteria. He knew I was having a bad day; it's easy to tell. If he wants me he can just come get me. I mean it. He is going to have to make every single move. I won't be taken advantage of again. I want to cry, but I can't.
I wish I didn't exist.
Every time I see my former boyfriend I want him, but I know it's not right. We aren't emotionally compatible. In fact, I'm not sure anyone is emotionally compatible with me. I've got too many feelings. How can I write down what I'm feeling when I don't know what I'm feeling? It's just misery is what I feel.

Later—

I'm home! ! It feels so good to be crawling into my own bed again. . . . I hated saying goodbye to Dave. Not so much being without him but the actual saying goodbye was a bit awkward. Last night he called and wanted to come over and talk. It was so much fun. I felt so completely content. All I wanted to do was make him happy. I'm not sure I was too successful which was a bit disappointing. I always want someone else's feeling to match mine, and that's not fair. Like I wanted him to feel as totally happy as I did and I was disappointed when things didn't quite work out that way. . . . Maybe I am just too demanding.
It's funny, sometimes I like Dave so, so much and other times I can just be without him. I'm independent. Like right now. Sure I wouldn't mind if he were

around, but I rather like my independence. I needed to be away from him this weekend to get a bit of perspective on our relationship. I don't want things to move too fast. It's so easy to let that happen. Last night, for instance, I felt so comfortable curled up in his arms. I wanted to stay like that. I wish I wouldn't feel that way. I mean I wish I wouldn't feel that I needed a guy. I want to be self-sufficient and to be able to get along without them, but I just can't. I need to be loved and appreciated by a guy. At least accepted for what I am.

I want Dave to meet my parents, but I don't know if anything will work out. I hope so!!

This afternoon I went to Mary's wedding. She's so lucky!! It made me want to get married so badly....

I am no closer to knowing how I feel now than I was a month ago, when I began writing this journal. It is so frustrating and confusing.

Back at college—

Sometimes I get mad at myself for liking affection. I don't want to get into any kind of habit with him where you are just touching for the sake of touching. I really am enjoying life these past few days. I'm just starting to realize that I have good relationships with about 25 or so guys. It's nice to just be able to talk with guys and not have to flirt with them, although I still do that sometimes. I'm beginning to realize that I really don't have to go out on dates to be friends. Guys around here are afraid of the implications of dating, afraid that the girl would get too serious. I'm not like that, at least I don't think I am.

I like the relationship I have with Dave. He's very, very special, but yet I'm free. I can talk with other guys and do things with them without feeling that I have to hide anything from him. And yet when we are together I'm completely satisfied. Like tonight, studying, I was just sitting on the floor beside him with my head on his arm. We studied like that. That was enough to make me completely happy.

He knows he's special.

....

I got a note from my former boyfriend yesterday. It said he was thinking about me and hoped I would find the kind of friends that would lead me toward God. It ended by saying that he hoped the next friend I found would be myself, and it was signed love, John.

I'm not quite sure how I feel about the whole thing. I was glad he wasn't resentful at all and it seemed as though he really did care about me. That made me feel good although I still tend to mistrust him. I guess that is only natural.

I do know I need God, but I am too stubborn to let myself go. I still think I can do it on my own and I can't. When will I learn? Dave, can you help me? I hope so.

The confusion of the identity struggle is ending for Linda. Her feelings have taken her on a roller coaster ride. She has been up and down, round and round, into darkness and into light. Then, finally, it all began to subside and she began to know who she was and she made a commitment.

Jim had come through a similar experience. He, too, went on that journey of excesses; feelings that ricocheted back and forth. The only difference is that he could not bring this stage to a closure with a clear knowledge of who he was. He had only bounced around in the confusion and then came out dazed, unable to say what he had learned, and thus unable to commit himself to a lifestyle.

After this, the two, Jim and Linda, go on two different psychological journeys: Jim into aimless despair; Linda into a clear sense of integrity. He was unable to take hold, but she took a firm grasp on life.

Every adolescent has his message and it should be heard. It is often hard to comprehend because of the intense and conflicting emotions. But, in the midst of it all, adolescents are clearly communicating. The art we need to learn is to hear what is being said by the language of emotions.

Here is more of Linda's journal.

Today has just been neat. I just have to write! ! Even though it is late. I've been extremely studious all day.... Anyway, I had a pretty long talk with Cindy. We talked about our relationship with God and she really encouraged me and made me feel good. Then, when she left, I talked to Dave and we agreed to get together tonight. I told God that tonight was all his and he was in control of the direction Dave's and my relationship took tonight. And you know things went so well. I just didn't have the strong desire to be touched like usual. He just took it all away. I just feel so relaxed and under his control. Thanks God!

Later—

God has been so good to me! I don't deserve any of it! ! I have a job this summer.... I got my old job at the store. It is just an answer to prayer, only I haven't prayed for it. I didn't know how I was going to keep busy all summer. I've been afraid I would be bored stiff and miss all my friends very much. Especially Dave! ! God is a step ahead of me, anticipating every move. It's a weird feeling, but very comforting and secure.

. . . .

Well, I'm here! ! His house is just as I expected and his family pretty much so also. . . . Dave is treating me just as I thought he would. In other words, I'm just a girl he brought home from college. . . .

Back at college—

Dave and I have been growing closer all the time. It's so neat. Sunday night on the way back we got a chance to talk. It straightened out many things, but also left much unsaid. We have to be in constant communication with God in order for our relationship to work. Saturday night was an example of what happens if God is excluded. It upset Dave more than me. Let me see if I can explain. To me a kiss doesn't mean as much as it does to him and so when we kiss each other we are saying two different things. We talked a lot about this and it really helped me in being able to understand him. When I kiss him I have to be careful not to do it just in fun, but only when I really want to show him how special he is.

I'm sure God put us together to teach each other. We have so much to offer each other. He can help me with my relationship with God and so teach me discipline and self-control. I want to be able to help him learn to be more expressive both emotionally and verbally. God really can use us if we just let him, but sometimes it is just so hard.

A month later—

Well, I am finished with my freshman year of college. It seems like the year has just started and now it's over. I can't believe I'm actually in college. I used to think college kids were so old and mature, but I know differently now.

It's also hard to believe that I'm not going to see Dave for three months. I've spent so terribly much time with him this past week. . . .

Later at home—

Dave, please come visit me. He wrote me the most fantastic letter yesterday. It made me feel so good. I hope we don't have any trouble communicating. . . .

The whole family was up until 11 o'clock watching the Flyers game. They won the Stanley cup for the second year in a row. It was funny to hear Mom and Dad get all involved in a hockey game.

Speaking of Mom and Dad, we are getting along well. Talking comes easy, there is so much to say. . . .

Sunday was another good day. I really got a lot out of Church and Sunday School. I joined the church's seekers class in preparation for church membership. . . .

Later on a visit to Dave's house—

Dear God, you have been so wonderful to me. I don't deserve any of it, but thank you anyway. It's so good to be with Dave again this weekend. Last night we talked and talked and straightened out any possible misunderstanding that could arise by only keeping in contact through letter writing.

Later—

It wasn't near as hard to say goodbye this time because I knew things hadn't changed by being separated. We felt the same towards each other. . . .

Later that summer—

Upon the confession of my faith in the Lord Jesus Christ I was baptized today. And guess what, I was the first to go up in the pulpit to give my testimony. . ."

At this point I will stop and describe how a girl like Linda has handled emotions in each stage—from before adolescence through young adulthood.

To listen to any child at each stage of development one must listen primarily to their emotions. It helps when one knows what to listen for.

While in the primary grades a child simply feels, without any particular awareness that she has her own emotions. She knows she may be rejected by her classmates and that hurts. She may cry, but her whole self-image is not at stake. A fond kiss or a moment of understanding by her parents heals all the pain.

The junior high era introduces the first occasion for a person to feel that all those emotions are part of himself. This is frightening at first, because it catches him off guard so often. One way to deal with it is to attack anyone who arouses deep feelings. The opposite sex has to be avoided with great effort because they trigger a whole host of absolutely new emotions. A person this age cannot cope with these because he hasn't even come to terms with the feelings that he cannot avoid.

As a person enters high school he now knows he must confront all these experiences; it cannot be delayed. He is so deeply preoccupied with his inner journey that parents get in his way. Often this means that he has to attack the roadblock, which happens to be his parents. Some boundaries in behavior have to be set and parents are the designated ones to do it. But in return they must expect to experience intense frustration and anger directed at them.

Gradually the primary task of working out the emotions shifts from parents to the peer group. Fortunately when Linda was ready for this task she also could legitimately be hundreds of miles away from her parents.

The final stage of adolescent development ends when the person can make a commitment. Linda, unlike Jim, was able to do this. In her case it was to God as her Savior, to college as a career, and to a select peer member as a potential mate. After that, she could return to meet her parents again. The adolescent journey has ended and she could return home.

Later, at nineteen years of age the following letters were exchanged with her parents:

Dear Family,

I really doubt whether I'll be home for Easter. Dave wants me to come to his home. That's too good an offer to refuse. We may end up coming home for part of the time either from here or his place. It's too far ahead to tell. I know you probably don't understand but it is really hard to keep our relationship growing with both of us too busy to have time here in school. Especially him—he is so busy. Vacation would be so good for us.

I don't want to hurt your feelings and make you feel like I'm taking advantage of you. I really do appreciate you sending me to school. Do I need to come home on vacation to show it? Please (especially Mom) let me know if you're hurt! I'm really getting independent.

It's never going to be the same. Dave's becoming more and more important to my future. We've started to talk a lot about marriage even though that is still in the distant future. It seems funny to say this, but neither of us questions if we'll get married. When seems to be the issue. I know I'm not even twenty yet but I do know what I want.

I'd hate to be a parent. It must be rotten to have your kids go running off as soon as you can finally communicate. I'm sorry about that, but it is part of growing up, right?

I hope Sue [her sister] finds a guy as good as Dave. I'm getting gushy again! It seems it always ends up like that.

I really do appreciate all the hard work that's been put into me over the years. It's scary to think about taking a dependent nothing of a baby and shaping him/her into an independent adult. I don't think I want that responsibility—yet.

I hope you know how much I love you, even though it isn't said. Somehow it's easier to tell Dave than you. So long.

Love,
Linda

The first message in the letter was one of pure joy that she experienced as her own sense of personhood came together so naturally. The raging emotions of adolescence have subsided and an inner peace is setting in. It is true that the soft hand of a lover helps a lot. But that is not all. She, too, is different. It is not the clinging, grasping desperation she exhibited for years before. She is now reaching out with a tenderness and a certainty that makes it possible for him to respond. And she feels whole.

The second voice is that of guilt. She has feelings about forsaking her parents for someone else. She has a few too vivid memories of her adolescence, when she at times drove her parents to despair. Then, she needed to go after every experience with total abandonment, hardly looking back to see what this did to her family. Now, she knows this phase is finished and, just as she is ready to meet them as adults, she hears the call to leave. This provokes guilt, but her parents released her of this. For they heard this deeper voice accurately and answered her letter.

Dear Linda,

It may surprise you to know that your stepping out so boldly into life away from us feels very good to us. As soon as we received your letter, mom read it aloud. We laughed at your eloquent way of describing your leaving us. Immediately afterwards we sensed a deep peace fall over us. You are telling us our job is done, and that feels good. It is not that we don't want you home for Easter, or near us at other times. It is only that we well know that you have a higher calling that you must go after. To know that you hear it accurately and are obedient is a far greater joy than the joy that any Easter dinner can provide, no matter with whom. So, go, girl, go.

Would you believe that your growth frees us to grow also? It helps us step into our next stage of development—the beginning of the post-parenting era. Not that it doesn't have its own fears with it, such as the simple reminder of the aging process, but it also is a deep liberating experience. For one, we are much more free to respond to each other instead of having to put the needs of children first, which we chose to do for twenty years.

Your separating seems so natural and so accurately timed. There was a time for you to be a child, when you needed us so desperately. There was a time for you to be a teenager, which you acted out vigorously enough. And now, it is time to take the next step, which you do with such silent certainty.

Not only is it beautiful to observe, it gives us the confidence that your younger brothers and sisters will follow. It is such an excellent example for them.

We would prefer that you not drive all those hundreds of miles out of your way to stop by here for the brief vacation you have. It would only disrupt the agenda that you know so clearly you should follow. So, please follow it! And we say that out of love for you also.

Sincerely,
Your Parents

Thanks, Linda. Thanks for sharing your journal with me so freely. And thanks, too, for all those who cannot speak as eloquently as you do, but who experience adolescence just as deeply. Your voice is the voice of many others.

And Linda, in case you don't already know, you are a very fortunate girl to have been heard now. Having been listened to also explains why you were able to navigate the river of adolescence, no matter how rough the rapids were, so successfully.

Difficult as it may be, adolescents need to be listened to as they cross this most stormy phase of their life. In the midst of the emotional turmoil an adult is emerging, if we can only hear that message behind all their noise.

5

JOE
Who Listens to Thrown-Away Mates?

Marriages break up like puppy loves used to. The statistics tell us that the million-per-year mark has long been passed. On certain days the column of "Divorces granted" is longer than the column of "Marriage licenses issued." Whether presidential candidates are divorced is no longer a political issue. There are weekly magazines that keep a running account of the disintegrating marriages of famous and infamous personalities.

It's all taken for granted. Everybody is doing it. So it means nothing to us any more. We are no longer moved by the worst. We are prone to yawn and say, "I could have predicted it. So what else is new?"

All of this is only the superficial truth. If we only knew what lies behind each scene. The hidden drama is often so excruciatingly painful that it ought to drive us to tears, if not to prayer.

Is anyone listening?

It was Sunday afternoon. I had really planned to take it easy. But then I got a telephone call from a client, a young twenty-seven-year old mother who could not endure the afternoon alone. Her husband of seven years had already told her that he no longer loved her and there was someone else. He had disappeared that afternoon without explanation but she knew he was with "the other woman." She had been crying and continued to do so. I wasn't sure I could be of any further help until their next appointment. I had let her cry and tell of her pain. One child was only three months old. The other was old enough to keep on asking, "Why are you crying mommy?" and then crawl on her lap to hug her. Even a young child tried to heal the pain.

"All right," she responded. "I'll take my children to the park across the street from your home. If you have a moment, come over to see me. If not, at least I'll know you are near."

Oh how dreadful! I cringed at the thought. This is the truth about the other side of the marriage situation —a broken human being hanging on to one thin thread for survival. To be a block away from someone who cared was the most there was for her.

Later on I slowly walked over to the park. Her head was leaning against her chest in deep sobbing. With one foot she slowly pushed a baby carriage back and forth. A tiny infant slept fitfully. An older one was busy trying out all of the playground equipment. I paused for a while. She didn't see me coming. I didn't want to startle her. Finally I said her name. She looked up and with a deep sigh said, "Oh thank God!"

What more could I say or do? I asked her to tell me about the children. I marveled at their beautiful innocence. To this she exclaimed, "I fear for their future. What will happen to them if I as a single parent am crumbling?" She told me over and over again all the facts of her husband's total rejection of her; of her endless attempts at reconciliation—all to no avail. Now here she was, at her wits' end and at the mercy of her fate.

JOE: *Who Listens to Thrown-Away Mates?*

Could I even risk letting her go home alone?

As another example I would like to share the firsthand account of Joe's "survival journal." This was not written for publication; not even for me to read. It was written only to cope—to make it one day at a time.

This journal became a rudder when a man lost all direction, and all other guides he knew were in shambles.

The moment he knew he had lost his wife of nine years to a lover, he began writing furiously. He could talk to his journal even if not to her. Only a fraction of the total written material is reproduced here. After it was finished he allowed me to read it.

When I asked to include it he helped me reproduce it by reading it into a tape recorder. Much of it was illegible because it was written with such intense and frantic emotions. It is too bad this attribute is lost in its reproduction.

Listen to the voice of a thrown-away mate screaming to survive and remain intact until divorce is final. Perhaps then he can start over again.

Sunday, December 14—

I don't really know why I'm writing this. Maybe it's so that years from now I can look back to remember, or to feel sorry, or to feel glad. I'm thinking that maybe one day I can show this to someone I love, or just to another person—anyone who is hurting—and show them how it goes, how it works itself out. Today I'm pretty sure it will work itself out. I can't guarantee that I won't cry anymore, inside or out. But to have gotten to this point is something in itself. I'll make it.

I feel so much right now that my thoughts run to-

gether. I can't write fast enough. Hope this will be legible even to me when I want to read it. Funny—I usually hate to write, but right now it feels good.

Let me go back. Last Saturday night I found the love letters (written to my wife by her lover). Before that I can't even describe it, just a jumble of emotions. (She loves me, she loves me not.) The scary part is knowing (?) someone for eleven years and finding out you knew nothing at all.

I'm worried—can I ever trust again?

I've got to—but . . . ?!

The letters—I read them all: "My darling Janice" . . . "All my love forever." The worst is hearing yourself talked about in the third person. "I don't believe it. He's changed his mind about the divorce," or "He's a zipless———."

I was numb.

Like reading a novel about some made-up situation and people.

I called her dad. Told him. I had to talk to him.

I knew I'd tell her that night.

I had still felt I could court her—make her see what I was and where I was at. No snow job or anything. I called the Sheraton Inn for a reservation for that night. I'd tell her there (about the letters). No distractions (kids, etc.).

Over dinner I wanted her to tell me. I tried to get her to see that I knew.

Maybe she did!

But no luck! I got the same story. "I want to be alone," and "I think I still love you!"

Wow!!

To the Sheraton Inn! Was she really pleasantly sur-

JOE: *Who Listens to Thrown-Away Mates?*

prised (that I took her out)? She was all set to make love to me.

How??

She got in bed. All smiles.

I took her hand and told her . . .

She blinked once. Kind of fast. That was it.

I was really afraid to scare her. I remember the feeling once when we came home . . . and saw an ambulance in front of our house. We thought it was our son. What a feeling!! That's how I was afraid for her.

Did I still love her or was it because she is just a person?

I hate it when people hurt. I almost got sick at the Sheraton after that. Actually, at first, I was kind of rational.

Maybe not! Maybe like that novel again. But after that I couldn't catch my breath.

I wasn't scared.

Kind of hoped I'd die right there in bed.

That would show her! Right?

Slept about one or two hours that night. Got up at seven thirty to take her to work. That was Sunday. I had to talk to her Dad.

Why?

I had to be with someone who loved (or at least liked) me and loved the kids. And he'd find out anyway. And I had to get out of the house.

Left with my boys at 9 A.M. Got to the house at 11:30. The kids were great. *I LOVE THEM!*

It was agony waiting for him to get home from church. Finally he did at 11:45. Then we ate. The time just dragged. It was all I could do to keep from crying right there. At last we went off to his office—1:30 or so.

CRY ! ! ! *That was all I could do.*
WOW! *I needed him.*
CRY! CRY! CRY!
We talked for two hours.
Mom came over. I even held her hand. What a pitiful mess! Then we left to go back to the house.
They called Janice. Waste of time.
Am I surprised! Sometimes I hate myself for being so dumb and naive.
I did the right thing, at least for me.
We left for home at 6:30. Kids were great again. GOD, *I'll miss them. I'll need help for that. Just for that—Now!*
Got home at 9 P.M.
No talk.
Didn't sleep much. Was a wreck at work!
Things get a little mixed up chronologically. When was the last time we made love? December 2 or 3, maybe. It's funny how or why it matters.
A small thing happened on 12/11. Funny how I care . . . how it means so much, such a big deal. Doris at the bank said it would get better, that she'd gone through it. The next day I went back to sign some papers. I gave her a rose. Dumb and sentimental!
Started getting practical:
  The lawyer
  Stocks
  Bank
  Take care of loveletters
  Cancel ski trip
  Calls (Mom and Dad in Florida)
  Airline reservation
  Called—Sue, Betsy, Dave, Karen, etc.
At last came Friday 12/12. Packed. Janice took me

to airport. *Good to be alone—to get out of Philadelphia. Felt sorry for myself. Slept some.*

Got to Miami. Couldn't talk to Mom and Dad. Lump in my throat. Probably too tired.

Got to apartment.

In bed. Had to cry!

I needed someone then. Dad came in, asked "Shall I stay with you?"

I said, "Yes." Wished he had put his arm around me, but I understood.

Took a Tranxene [tranquilizer] *and fell asleep.*

What a great feeling to wake up the next morning, December 13.

Mom and Dad were good.

I ran to the stores near the beach.

Had to run!

Still do!

The pain is good. Physical pain. It's good therapy.

Bought some sneakers, belt, post cards for kids.

Ran back.

Went to beach. I needed a girl . . . The worst part is losing your self-confidence. I never had much, especially concerning my physical appearance. I talked to three or four girls. No luck. Bad lines I guess. Worse for my confidence.

Ran up the beach and back, about two miles, I guess.

Felt good to lie on the beach.

The physical change really helps to make you forget. Temporary though. I'm afraid of going back. Drove back to apartment.

Slept. Still needed a girl.

Went out to bar. Scene is . . . poor.

Loud drunk.

Cheap portrait.

Organ player . . .
Came back to apartment at 11:30.
Had three drinks—so just slept.
No Tranxene for over twenty-four hours now.
Good!
Will need them for New York. How will I make it? ? ? The two weeks she is going to spend with her lover?
Morning again! Yea! !
I hate the night! ! Have awakened to vomit almost every night.
Fixed the bicycle and left for beach.
No dumb lines. Just lay there.
The wind and the sun felt good. The sand stinging when the wind gusted.
Got dressed. Rode up to Sunny Isles. More pain? Not really, just rode slow.
One note: I notice things more now. Flowers, weeds, clouds. Also families, couples. That hurts.
Bought goggles.
Rode back to apartment.
Got there just in time to go out on yauht. Oh, heck! How do you spell that word? Skipper was 32. I climbed up on the flying bridge to talk. It was great. Told him a lot. What does it matter? He told me a lot. People mean more to me now too. It's about time.
I don't think I'll forget.
LIVE!

. . . .

Back from boat.
Will learn to listen. To pay attention. People count.
Ten fast laps in pool.

Pain.
Get in shape.
Don't forget.

....

Started writing. I'm no poet, but I'm thinking of things that are kind of neat.

A tiny bird (sparrow I think) saw me sit and eat and came right up and looked me in the eye, "Food, please."

Later an old lady walked by me, saw me come and as I passed she turned her head away—Ouch.

I'm searching now!

I know I'll never be the same, but how much will I change?

Mom proposed that I check into medical schools. I'm intrigued! I don't think I can be what I am now, all my life, but I'm scared. Thirty years old! Can I do it? I love to help people. It would be neat to be a pediatrician. Kids are great!! But it must be tough to see them hurt. If you can help them, that's the high. If you can't, it must hurt like hell. If one dies how can you stand it?

I'm afraid.
I need confidence.
I must take the initiative.
Janice is out! out! **OUT!**
Lies!
Deceit!
Is she sick?
If she does an about-face in the next month or two I must resist.
I need lots of time now.
Can't be afraid. . . .
More tomorrow.

Wish it were tomorrow morning. If I could just get through the night, from the time I lay down in bed until tomorrow morning. . . .

The night is absolutely the worst time! That dream over and over. . . . Like in the horror movies where the girl gets killed in the end and turns into a monster before your eyes.

Monday, December 15—

Yea!! Morning.

Had to take a pill to sleep. Was a little apprehensive about calling a school.

I've got to make a list of what to do when I get back to New Jersey.

Right now it seems to all fall into place. How will I feel when the weather is cold and I'm back under pressure?

The list:

  (1) Join YMCA
  (2) Move out of house
  (3) Set up a nice bachelor pad
  (4) Be good to people
  (5) Try!

Called school, the list of undergraduate courses is staggering! Must do it one step at a time. Maybe take chemistry first.

Can I do it on top of the divorce and all?

Nite now.

Tuesday, December 16—

At beach now, used a good line and talked to an Eileen for about an hour.

JOE: *Who Listens to Thrown-Away Mates?* 119

She's screwed up too. 28 years old. Divorced. No direction.
I guess I'm better off.
Rode bike to Sunny Isle, across Causeway, down Boulevard, across Bay Harbour Isles.
Tired . . .
Called Janice.
Talked to kids.
I LOVE THEM!
I just listened.
Trite.
Stupid.
I was cold.
What could I say?
Damn night again. Took pills. Will read now and try to sleep. I still think I've got it together. Afraid of returning to New Jersey and New York. More tomorrow!

Wednesday, December 17—

Problem: Telephone tape recorder had a message which may have been from Janice. (Probably was.) Can't figure it out. Said to call her . . .
Sounded cold?
Verge of tears?
Why?
Will wait for her to return call.
Options:

(1) Kids sick, hurt?
(2) She wants to tell me Dec. 27 is off?
(3) Something came up with lawyer, finances?
(4) She's leaving with kids?

That's all I can think of. Am apprehensive.

Back from a date—now I'm scared again. She's just a girl—a woman—29 years old—younger than me. But she's old. And single.
How will I end up? 6 months from now?
One year? Ten years?
I'm scared.
Meanwhile Janice called here—talked to Mom. Called to ask about car registration! That's meaningless.... She was angry, bitter, even to Mom. Wow!
Sick?
It's out of my hands now!
Out of my mind!

Friday, December 19—

Mom and Dad arguing is really getting to me now! I'm really upset now about going back next Tuesday. Must tell Brandt (my oldest son) what's going on. But how? ? ?
Help!
Went to small airport in afternoon. Told guy I'd like to sky dive, that I'd done it before.... He said OK ... no big deal.

Saturday, December 20—

Very depressed.
Ran four miles.
Swam in pool.
Home to apt. for T.V.
Hope I can sleep.
Afraid to go back home. (What home?)

Sunday, December 21—

Very bad day.

JOE: *Who Listens to Thrown-Away Mates?*

Depressed.
To beach. Ran couple of miles. To apartment. Back to beach. Played volleyball. No fun . . .
Ate too much.
Bowled.
Tried to work it out of me.
I was mad.
I'm a little afraid of my anger now. Dreamed I was trying to hit Janice but couldn't. The dreams are frightening . . . Screaming . . . Vomiting . . .
Trouble sleeping!

Tuesday, December 23—

Eleven thirty A.M. *now. About to leave for airport.*
Bad scene last night. Janice called to say she had stopped checks from stocks.
Drank, went to bed at 8:30.
Slept till 1:30 A.M.
Took 2 pills.
No luck.
Read.
Tried to sleep.
Finally slept till 8:30.
Called lawyer.
Feel better.
Let's see how it goes now?

Later—

On plane now (to New Jersey).

Wednesday, December 24—

Tomorrow is big day. (Christmas)
Hope all holds up—Me!

Thursday, December 25, Christmas morning—

Bad, Bad, Bad!
Yesterday got home.
Left for New York.
Got kids there in time for manger service.
God!
How bad.
Hanging stockings!
Shallowness!
Pain!

Friday, December 26—

Awful day.
More of same.
Decided I couldn't cope with kids while Janice shacks up.
Am going skiing.

Saturday, December 27—

Drove to Vermont.
Tough trip.
Was Janice at our home with her lover? in our bed? next to her?
My mind racing with the thought.
Why does that part hurt so much?

Monday, December 29—

Last night was scary as hell.
Tired, stayed up too late.
Two pills.
Good sleep.
Thank God.

JOE: *Who Listens to Thrown-Away Mates?* 123

During day skied alone. . . . Was bad on Nosedive. I got very angry at myself for doing bad like that.

Thursday, January 1—

Wow!
What a kaleidoscope of events!
Am I losing my mind or drowning it in confusion?
Back in New York.
My son—nice!
Went for walk with him.
At dinner he asked, "Daddy, when you move to another house, can I see you whenever I want?"
Wow!
Had a good cry!
Needed two pills to sleep.
Left for New Jersey today. Checked out house. Relaxing now.
Scared of nite.
Appointment with Dr. Schmitt tomorrow at 4:00— Need help!

Saturday, January 3—

Yesterday was a great day.
What a high!
I've got it made now.
Saw Janice—didn't phase me.
Saw Dr. Schmitt—Good session.

Thursday, January 8—

Amazing—there are such extreme ups and downs.
Got called a "Disneyland daddy" by Janice.
Janice is a bitch.
Slept well!

Tuesday, January 13—

Not much time to write now—Busy as hell! Overdid it a little this weekend.

Oh! ... I got into a course at the university—General Chemistry II. Preparation for Organic.

I'm scared.

Janice told me again she's on the verge of giving me the kids. I want them now. A lot!!

I pray this works out.

Sunday, January 18—

I feel so good about myself. . . . I'll make it in school, work is going good.

I've got this Janice thing all sorted out in my head.

Hopes for kids—

For Grad. School—

For myself.

People like *me*!!!

And I like myself!!!

Monday, January 19—

It's 8:00 A.M. now.

Fed the kids breakfast.

I love them so, so much!!

I just want to be the best daddy I can.

Must maintain my energy to handle all this.

I think I can.

Is this confidence or conceit?

It really doesn't matter now.

Will study today.

It's great to be alive!

JOE: *Who Listens to Thrown-Away Mates?*

Tuesday, January 20 (8:30 A.M.)—

Monday (yesterday) was a neat day. My head was so clear and felt so warm.

First lab at university was bad.

Got me really worried.

Am I cut out for this Med School thing? Maybe I'm kidding myself—just using the Med School route as a way of giving myself a future that I can control, instead of being at the mercy of others. We'll see....

Class again tonight.

Hope I catch on.

Thursday, January 22 (9:00 A.M.)—

Drove all the way down to university Tuesday nite.

Snow—ice.

No class.

Talked to a girl (woman) with 4 kids. Married to a lawyer. Nice!

She told me about her friend whose husband left her —pregnant, 2 kids—really in bad shape after 6 months. I felt awful. She suggested we all get together over dinner.

I must try to help.

I got over my agony in 6–7 weeks. My God!!!

Six months of hell.

Must help.

If I can.

Waitress was kind to me as she served me. I almost felt guilty about it. Funny how Janice has trained me not to expect things like that.

Is strange how our marriage eroded like that—little by little.

So it was unnoticeable day by day. Like having your hair turn gray and not realizing it until you look at a picture taken 5 years ago.

Must be careful!

Think—Joe!

Don't just let emotions tell you what to do.

Too many things at stake.

The boys!

My career!

My life!

I'm only going to live once and time is too precious.

Don't make another wrong turn and lose the time doubling back.

Will see Dr. Schmitt tonight. He wants to see this journal. I'm somewhat embarrassed. I haven't even read it myself. Must get to work.

Joe, I want to teach others to listen with love. You know that is how I listened and it made a difference to you. Even as you read this I know you will agree with me.

The first point I wish to make comes out of your readiness to share your journal with me, and then to gladly have me use it for publication.

Remember how you exclaimed, "If this will help someone, maybe something good will come from all this mess." I hear your fear of total despair screaming at me. When life caves in, there is always the danger of collapsing and giving up.

All of those many months I knew you, and as you repeatedly stated in your writings, you panicked at the thought that you would surrender to hopelessness. This was your greatest fear. Then, when I wanted your journal, you began to see some purpose in all of this suffering. At least it could be translated to some worth.

There are over a million people out there somewhere whose marriages are going down the drain this year alone. "Could any of them be helped if they knew how much I hurt?" you asked.

I also hear you wondering if you aren't extremely abnormal to care this much about Janice. "After all," everyone says, "You'll love again. There are many eligible women around. How dare you grieve in agony when mates are swapped like chairs in that famous game?"

That makes it all the worse. It has become a norm in our society to discard mates like you dispose of last year's car model for the latest and the best.

I hear your body also pleading for attention. This had been such a natural and beautiful part of your life, and suddenly it was all gone. Your yearning turned to fantasy and you began pursuing it as if it were real. Then you began doubting your maleness. After all, to be so abruptly discarded by someone you meant to keep forever devastates any ego. Then, perhaps yours wasn't that strong to begin with. No wonder you began to try to prove that your masculinity was still intact. I do not agree with your behavior, but I do accept your longing. I do understand the deprivation.

Suddenly you began to hear other people in pain, and you cared more than most of us do. You even noticed a tiny bird, and you heard it say, "Food, please." Now that is sensitive listening. How carefully you monitored the feelings of your two boys! You knew their pain. You were suffering with them.

I hear you yearning to help others, even to return to a pre-medical curriculum and then go on to medical school so as to be in a helping profession. Granted, you might be doing it to prove your self-worth to yourself; but to have such a compassionate pediatrician would be great. You may care for my children, or my children's children, any time. I believe you would cringe at every sight of pain, but, at least, you would know that a hypodermic needle hurts.

There is much regret in your voice, Joe. You call yourself naive. You say that you should have known long ago that your marriage was disintegrating, but then you sensitively compare it to hair turning gray. It happens so slowly that you don't even notice.

I also hear a new man emerging out of this debris—a very sensitive person. You even notice an old lady walking by and, when she deliberately turns her head away, you exclaim, "Ouch."

What more is there to listening than to feel pain when someone says "Ouch?"

6

MELISSA
The Voice of a Sharecropper in Graduate School

No one could have known the transformation that Melissa's presence in this class would cause. Only vaguely do I remember any other student, but her beautiful black face remains vivid in my memory.

My first sight of her was when she took the farthest seat to the rear of the classroom. As I asked the students to introduce themselves and cite some interesting facts of their field placement or life experience, she barely responded. She made only a quick statement of her name, a few facts, and then she pulled into herself in embarrassment. She was obviously overwhelmed.

I momentarily cringed at this behavior. "My! Does she ever think little of herself. Does she not know that there is more to say that is important? Has something happened to her?" I could not ask since it would embarrass her only more. So I passed her by, but made a mental note that she would need some special attention later this semester. She is hurting, I thought, and all must hear this hurt.

Students taking a master's degree program in social work are usually inquisitive, intelligent, and eloquent. Thus, the mood of this class was optimistic as they expressed their good feelings about having successfully completed the first of four semesters. Now they were beginning the second and were eager to proceed.

After this general introduction of the students was completed, I turned to define the purpose of this course.

Family Dynamics, as this class was called, is a fancy title for studying the family. Its purpose is to understand the subtle inner pulls and pushes that affect family living. It is also to study the unique atmosphere of a kinship group of people that changes as the seasons of the year change. To this climate the professionals attribute the basis for the formation of personality variations in children and adults. The family can be studied to understand how people nurture each other so that its members will fulfilled and grow to wholesome adulthood and old age. It can also be used to understand the forces that mutilate and devastate certain people, and then to discover ways of halting this and translating it into a healing process. This was essentially our task for the semester.

I proposed a method of study that brought many positive responses. The key task for every student was to do as complete a "dynamic analysis" of his or her family life as possible. Each was to trace his own lineage backwards and sideways as far as was now significant to understand their present personality.

This meant that they were going to explore their family tree in order to discover the truths it could offer them about what made them uniquely themselves. This was all to be charted on a large wall model, so that each person could present the entire discovery to the class. The rest of us would then help in analyzing all the material.

Again there was a positive reaction. Students had often thought of doing this before, but now was their

MELISSA: *The Voice of a Sharecropper*

golden opportunity. Melissa was busily recording the information on the assignment. When she did glance up, she looked distraught.

Soon the class was in full swing. Week after week eager students took turns in inviting us into their innermost life. Many profound discoveries were made about the effect of specific events upon the student as well as general discoveries about what makes families do what they are doing to each other.

One particularly fascinating presentation was done by a Jewish girl. As she unfolded her huge chart before the class, our eyes all fell immediately upon the thick vertical line at about the midpoint, with the lettering, "Nazi Holocaust, 1940–1945" written next to it. Dozens of lineage lines branched out like a tree, but almost all of them ended at the black line. Only two thin lines penetrated the barrier, and after this there was the beginning of another set of branches. At a glance we knew what the most dramatic event of her family tree was. This was a fact that deeply affected her since the day she was born. To support this, she began her presentation by simply saying that she had no relatives except her immediate siblings, since her parents were the only ones to survive the war.

She then told us of the effect the creation of the chart had upon her family. Night after night, for the last several weeks, her parents joined her to help her recreate her heritage. It became an experience of mutual grief that they had never faced before. They concluded that the war totally wiped out their past, and the past had always been so important to the Jewish community. Even the genealogies that were passed on from generation to generation were all lost. Because of this, they said, they had given birth to six children, more than most of their friends had. This would help begin a new family tree in the new world.

The student also concluded that it helped her understand her parents' persistent expectation that she marry early and have children soon. There was also a lot of pressure to succeed. She said that this was why she felt so compelled to make the best grades in college and then be admitted to an Ivy League university. It all made sense to her now, like never before.

One night as the whole family was together, again working on the chart, the father leaned back and said, "You know, children, I should have done this long ago with you. I just couldn't face it. It just brought back too awful memories for me. But this is exactly what my father and grandfather did with us. They traced our ancestors over and over again. Then they told us of the children of Israel wandering in the Wilderness, and finally entering the promised land. This was always part of serving the Passover. It has been too painful for me to go to the synagogue or keep the holy days, but now I know we must. This year we are going to have the Passover at our house."

"And I know he will," she added.

My mind now drifted. This is what education should be doing. It ought to change people, even the families of students. If only we could do much more listening to the lives of our students, rather than talking about our thought process, it would happen. Far more profound discoveries can be made in the souls of students than in most professors' heads.

At this point a black student who had thus far not said a word in class was deeply moved by this presentation and spoke: "You know we are very much like you are. Our history was also wiped out, only a hun-

MELISSA: *The Voice of a Sharecropper* 133

dred years earlier. When we were dragged out of Africa as slaves, we also lost our roots. We, too, still have many scars from it."

At this moment I noticed that Melissa wiped away a tear, though she said nothing.

I had a deep yearning to relate to her and other silent class members as I began: "Over the years of teaching, I have made a very meaningful discovery. In every class there are the outspoken, courageous students who get much of the floor time. I value them because they keep the class functioning, but I also know that the silent members have a different and very valuable contribution to make. Since both are necessary I frequently ask all students who have spoken several times in my class to remain silent for blocks of time. Often the deepest truths are known only by the others. Their silence is frequently due to their acute sensitivity and perceptivity that seems too precious to scatter in a noisy room. These contributions are often deeply intuitive rather than logical, and thus of a different quality."

Then I noticed that Melissa glanced up at me, as if I had defined her. I said, "Melissa, does that free you to say something?"

"Yes," she said, "I believe my presentation should be next. I, too, discovered that what happened in my history made an impact upon who I am. I am ready to do it next week."

I caught her before she left the classroom. I had received a note this past week from her faculty advisor stating that she was failing her whole clinical practice and that she would not get credit for this year, except in the courses that she completed successfully during the first semester. She told me that she already knew it, but she wanted to make the class presentation anyway. I had to tell her that I had responded to the advisor by telling him that she had volunteered nothing, that I had no idea who she was or what she had done in my class. "I know" she said, "that's what I want you to understand next week."

I was startled by the confidence of this girl, since I had sensed her extreme reluctance and withdrawal. She then added that this is exactly the way she had been in her field agency, and this was why she had failed. She stated she had come to a startling awareness in this class, but it is all too late.

The following week when we arrived in class a ten-foot chart was taped on the chalk board. Melissa, dressed in her finest, was near the head of the class waiting.

A deep silence engulfed the classroom as the students drifted in and began studying the chart. I did likewise. I felt like we all needed to get the full impact of the enormous amount of work that had gone into the creation of this chart.

On the far left she had printed the word, "Africa." After that, she shaded in the whole area which ended abruptly at a line marked "Proclamation of Emancipation, 1864." Then came a whole network of lineage lines marking the many branches that composed her family tree. This whole area was captioned with the word "Sharecropper." Then again, there was another vertical line, after which she wrote the word "Free." Scattered over the entire area were pictures: some, cut out of *National Geographic* magazine, of African huts. There were newspaper and magazine pictures of dozens of famous black people, and then family photos on the far left.

MELISSA: *The Voice of a Sharecropper*

After approximately ten minutes of reverent silence, I said, "Melissa, I believe you have something to tell us yet."

With confidence she said, "Yes, I do!" as she took her place at the head of the class to describe her family dynamics from an unknown beginning in another continent until the present.

Over a map of Africa she had drawn a large question mark. This she said was the first thing one needed to know to understand her and her people. "We do not know where we really come from. All we know is that hundreds of tribes were raided and I could be from any of them."

Next, she cited the fact of slavery as being an issue that always stayed with her. It was a universal message that blacks were inferior because of the skin color and because of their life style. "That message is deeply ingrained in our unconscious by our parents, our peers, and our playmates."

Then, with eloquence she said, "You cannot know me unless you know what blacks have suffered. You must remember we have not forgotten slavery. We cannot forget it as long as we are treated as inferior."

Another black student chimed in, "You must not forget that even if some of us are now treated as equals we still have deep feelings of inferiority that will not go away in one generation. That, we hope to minimize with our children."

"But you must also take in account," she continued, "that there were many great black people in our heritage. Even though they were not our blood relatives, they are our kin. That's why these pictures are on this chart. We identified deeply with them. They gave us the courage to overcome great obstacles."

She pointed to the picture of the Reverend Martin Luther King, with the words under it, "I have a vision." Then she added, "His vision became my vision. Someday I shall arrive at the Promised Land that he saw afar off. Then we shall be free, too."

She then described her whole family tree, which showed many subdivisions since the families were large. She also called our attention to the many short twigs all over the chart, which indicated the high rate of infant mortality.

A student asked her if that had any psychological meaning to her. Again she was ready for it. "Yes, it does. It always gave me the feeling that since my ancestors and I were spared, then I must live my life with purpose. I am alive, so I must make it count. So many others didn't even have a chance."

The "sharecropper" notation gave students a problem. This again she said has to be understood carefully. Then she showed all the family members who never escaped the "sharecropper" life. This included almost all her ancestors, as well as almost all her living kin. She noted, "It is a 'bondage of poverty' that very few escaped." For the few lines that penetrated that barrier she cited a specific person.

One of these lines which she pointed to was marked with a gold star and had a picture of an elderly black lady near by. "This star," she said, "is symbolic of my aunt, my gold star aunt who gave me the courage to get an education. She is the only one in my entire family who ever went to college. The picture is not my aunt, but is Mary McLeod Bethune, the founder of the college for poor blacks in Daytona Beach, Florida, where my aunt went to school. When my aunt came home she kept on talking and talking about Miss

MELISSA: *The Voice of a Sharecropper*

Bethune and the vision she had for blacks to get educated. That gave me the nerve to do it too."

From the chart, under the picture, she read Miss Bethune's words from her last will and testament. "I am aware that it (death) will overtake me before the greatest of my dreams—full equality for the Negro in our time—is realized." Then she picked up a wall motto that her aunt gave her as a little child. It also contained a quote from the college president. "Faith in God is the greatest power, but great too, is faith in oneself."

"As a child these words gave me the courage to try to escape the slavery of poverty of my family," she added.

She then pointed to the one thin line that penetrated the area beyond the "sharecropper" zone. "This is me. I am the only one in my family to escape. My first step was to a high school as I lived with my aunt in a nearby town. I felt terribly out of place because my clothes were so poor, and also my accent told everyone that I came from the country. Then, the next phase was when I went off to college. Since that was an almost totally black college I felt a lot better, but I had to study hard because of my poor academic background."

She called attention to the photo of a small shack on cement blocks. "This is the two-room house where I was born and where my parents still live. It is rented and sitting on a small plot of land from which they make a living, sharing the produce with a white landlord. They barely make a living."

A student in utter amazement exclaimed, "You mean to tell us that you are only one step removed from a sharecropper existence?"

"Yes," she said, "that is exactly what I'm trying to show you."

Then I pointed to the line that indicated her, and asked her why the line became dotted instead of a solid line, and also why she had a question mark at the end. I sensed that this was the exact right time to ask her. She had taken almost the entire class period and simply spellbound the class in her own life drama. Often students called attention to her courage to push ahead alone, against all odds. They were deeply moved by the magnificent chart and her profound understanding of her life story and all the dynamics that were involved.

She knew exactly what I was hinting at, and I was giving her clearance to tell her story now. This class needed to know.

"The line is broken because I was told only a week ago that I could not go on in this school because I failed my field practice and my practice class."

An exclamation came from the classroom, "What did you say?"

"I have failed my first year of graduate school. I want you to understand that, from the day I began classes and field practice, I have been overwhelmed. I was too frightened by this university. You don't know what it feels like; I was simply immobilized. My advisor, here at the school, did all he could to encourage me. My supervisor was the best possible, but it all did no good. I simply could not do the work that was required of me."

"But what about the other courses, like this one?" someone insisted.

"Well, I do get credit for several courses that I completed in the first semester. When the expectation was to do book learning and writing papers, I could do it. I was an excellent student in college. This semester I have completed very little, and as far as this course is concerned, I leave it to Dr. Schmitt."

Then, an alert student asked, "Melissa, you have not volunteered one remark in this class. Yet from your presentation, you know exactly what is going on in this class. I would even go so far as to say that your insights into your family dynamics are the best that we have seen until now. You took us far beyond your simple family and moved into the whole historical constellation including the whole drama of the black way of life, and showed how all this converged upon your unique journey. Don't you know that?"

"My head does, but my soul does not," she replied.

"Then you don't exactly believe Miss Bethune's motto about 'faith in yourself.'"

"Let me tell you something. All the while I was struggling to get my education, my mother kept on telling me, 'Melissa, don't do it. You are only going to get hurt.' When I came home crying after a failure, or after an embarrassing episode about my poor clothes, or I didn't understand something, she would add, 'Melissa, I told you we black folk don't belong out there. Why don't you stay among us? I don't want to see you hurt. The farther you go, the worse it will become.'"

"Are you now saying that your mother was right? Is the fact that you failed a sign that you should not have gone? Are you finally devastated in your educational journey?"

Large tears welled up in her glossy eyes as she said quietly, "Yes, I should have listened to her."

"Then you should return to the sharecropper way of life?"

"What else can I do?" she sobbed.

A deep sense of helplessness pervaded the classroom. No one dared speak, and I chose to remain silent too. There was a message in the silence of this room that was screaming to be heard. I wanted this class to hear it and never forget it. I wanted them to learn to listen to voiceless voices—that situations are crying out to be heard. No one listens to these. They are too busy talking. That is a good way to disguise the message that no one really wants to know.

When a student became restless and began, "I'd like to change the subject . . ." I quickly interjected, "Please don't. The subject is painfully obvious. I don't think we are ready to even talk about it. Until we are, let us remain silent."

Melissa sobbed quietly. Finally, in the midst of tears she blurted out. "I don't want to go back as a failure. I want to go back as a social worker to help my people. I have a husband and two children in the elementary school here in the city. It was so terribly hard for them to adjust to Philadelphia. The children found urban education baffling. Because of this, I often walked them to school. That is why I was late for this class and also why I missed time at the agency.

"My husband was unemployed for two months at the beginning of the year. He is an auto mechanic, but no one believed him, how good he was, because he worked only in a rural garage before. Now, they all like it here and want to stay."

Then an alert black male student rose to the occasion. "Melissa! Do you really want the master's degree in social work?"

"As much as I ever wanted anything."

"Is your husband behind you?"

"Yes he is."

"Couldn't you reapply next year, now that your family is settled and you won't have to go through the whole adjustment process? I believe you will not have to repeat several courses in the first semester, and you deserve credit for this course if you stick it out to the end."

"Yes!" I added, "I would encourage you to continue this class through to the end, even if it's the only course you take. I will write a full report of your class performance today and forward it to your school advisor, and also continue to do so through to the end if you choose to remain involved."

"Oh, thank you," she exclaimed. "You are so kind."

She then continued, "My advisor has asked me to reapply for next year. I am offered a job at my agency immediately because my supervisor believes I can be of special help to the black adolescent girls from the ghetto. This would give me a good beginning before school starts again."

"Then, what is really your problem?" came a voice from the back of the room.

She covered her face for a while, as she continued weeping, then, finally, said, "I'm afraid! I don't think I belong here. We should go back!"

I again signaled the class to remain silent. No words were now needed.

After a while a tall, poised student rose to her feet and walked confidently to the front of the class where Melissa was seated. She had heard the message accurately. She embraced Melissa and cheek to cheek began weeping also, then said: "Melissa, we love you. We want you to stay. Come back to school as soon as you can. You are so strong and so courageous. You have been a model to us. How powerful a will you have to survive, and how compassionate a heart you have for your people. Please don't let them down."

Melissa uttered, "I will try again."

As the student returned to her seat, I waited for a while then added: "The lesson we learned today goes far beyond family dynamics. There is nothing more I can add to it. You are dismissed."

The student body mobbed Melissa. I saw many embraces and heard many remarks.

"Come on Melissa, you can do it just as well as I."

"After all the hurdles you have overcome . . ."

"Your presentation was profound."

"You are a fantastic person."

Or simply, "I love you."

After all the students had left, she slowly drifted to me. "Why did you take the whole class period just for me? You never did that before."

I responded spontaneously, "Because you are you. Is that not enough?"

"No, it isn't," she said, "I don't understand."

"Let me repeat: you are a unique human being, like everyone else in this room, and you deserved all of our time for the whole period if you needed it. We heard your cry and we responded. It happened to take that long to get the full message."

"Wait a minute," she came back, "this is a class that is meant for every student in the classroom, not for helping one student alone."

"Okay, Melissa. You do need a full explanation. What happened in this classroom today was for every student here, not just for you.

"First of all, you must remember that you were the most withdrawn and silent member of this class. You had a big effect on this group by your silence. I'm sure students felt bewildered by what was happening to you. They didn't know what to do about it. To be an effective social worker one has to hear such silent suffering even though no utterance is heard. I saw you in the corner and I already knew, from the way you stole into the class, that you were in trouble. I tried several times to involve you directly, but each time you shriveled up more. Within myself, I said, 'Wait until the right day and I will use the occasion to show these students how to do it.' Today was my day.

"For the students it was a day of reconciliation. Their hurt for not being able to touch an abandoned class member was healed today. We all righted a wrong, here, in the classroom.

"I also wanted them to discover the art of accurately listening to suffering. Under my direction, with a real person, I wanted to show them exactly how to do it. They all will be better social workers because of it. They all accurately heard the voice of a silent student in the far corner of the classroom and cared for her until there was healing, like a group of social workers ought to do. Now thousands more out in the world will be better off because, hopefully, they cannot leave the silent suffering masses alone. That, in my assessment, is my job as a teacher. You helped me do it. Thanks a lot!

"As for me, Melissa, I am the more for this experience. My gift has been reaffirmed today. I have long ago discovered that, aside from anything else I may do, my most central reason for being is to listen sensitively to hurting humanity wherever it is appropriate. Today, it was right to do it in the classroom, for both you and all the students to experience.

"You see, you were hurting because of all that has

happened to you. But you must remember that your hurt, through your withdrawal, was hurting them also. Today I helped heal it for all. That confirms my 'call.'

"My primary task for existence is simply 'That which you do unto the least of these my brethren, you do unto me.' As you know, this is from the Bible. So I teach for God; I care about people for God; but primarily, I listen with love for him. Then, I take it one step farther and say—that is God's will for me. It is as simple as that. Today a need arose by your presence and I responded and God's will was done."

"That is simply beautiful. You make it so simple," she continued. "I already heard from the students that you once prepared for the ministry, so I felt that your responding to people was a result of your faith."

"No question about it, Melissa. I have to live for God. That gives me an ultimate reason for being. He also enables me to care for people. If all this were for myself alone, I couldn't. I'd give up in despair.

"Melissa, have you consulted God about your next move?" I queried.

"I have felt so strongly that I was led all the way through high school and college, and even when I was accepted here with the scholarship. But when I was hit by all this—I didn't tell you about my husband's discouragement when he was unemployed, and my children's illness. It was all too much and I lost my hold. Today I received a new vision. I know it will be a tough road but God is able to see me through. I will not abandon ship now and go back to Georgia."

Situations have voices. When they are crying they can be heard and someone ought to respond. If no one will, the people who were hurt by it will continue to suffer, generation after generation.

MELISSA: *The Voice of a Sharecropper*

Sometimes we respond to individuals who are in need without realizing that they are only symptoms of the real problem, which is much bigger than the individual. We may become discouraged because all our caring gives only temporarly relief as the chronic problem persists.

To look for the entire problem, the greatest issues, and to hear them even though no audible voice is defining them, is what I call listening to the voiceless voices of situations. If one then responds appropriately real healing can take place.

To hear Melissa requires listening to her whole life experience. The largest attribute of her situation was the fact of her blackness—all that ever happened to her personally, all the ancestors who preceded her. She bore the scars of history on her soul. The class heard this voice accurately with the help of a very persistent and courageous student who could articulate it clearly. Blackness causes situational pain that is devastating people. As we respond to individuals we must bear in mind that this is not sufficient until the fact of racism is also dealt with.

Poverty, illiteracy, and sharecropper existence are issues that need to be given voices. When Melissa confronted the expectations of a sophisticated professional training program in an Ivy League university these attributes of her background immobilized her and she gave up. She was ready to flee to the world of her childhood for safety. Once the class could hear this voice crying, they could respond to her correctly. They then did not see a coward who could not dare to try again, but a hero who had fought against unbearable odds and prevailed. Granted, she could not now take the next step no matter how strong she was. She could, with their support, regroup her courage, slow down her pace, and then start again. We are confident that on the next try she will succeed.

We need to look beyond the person and see the larger issue which is much more devastating than the fact that an individual may not have enough to eat. It is simply not enough to hear the cry of a hungry person and then give him food. We need to listen to the system that causes such inequality and respond to it so that more equal distribution of resources can be made. When we do that, we hear the cry of the situation which also needs hearing. Listening with love includes this dimension.

7

ALBERT
*A Life That Might
Have Been Heard*

He is only sixty years of age. For the past two decades he has been a key executive in a large corporation and financially very successful. It took long hours of hard work—total commitment to achieve this position and to hold on to it the way he did.

But now he is deeply depressed and looks ten or more years older than his chronological age. As he sinks his huge tired body into the sofa of my office, he looks like he would rather fall asleep forever than struggle once more. Life is too much for him and he is overwhelmed. As soon as I reached out to him, to ask about the previous week, tears welled up in his eyes. "If I had known that I would end up in a shrink's office at this stage of life, crying, I would have given up long ago."

My gut feeling is that of sadness, overwhelming sadness. This describes his whole demeanor, his mood, and his life.

But how can it be? He has made the mint he struggled to get: a beautiful huge rancher in the country; a pilot's license and a new Bonanza plane at a nearby airport. "You know it's the Cadillac of them all, the one with the V tail, with the best of communication equipment," he told me.

When he talked about flying, he perked up. He became more alive than at any other time. He was extremely well-versed in everything related to flying, including weather, the terrain of the land, the mechanism of planes, as well as flying skills. "You are a walking encyclopedia of flying knowledge," I told him.

My fascination with his flying momentarily brought him out of his depression. He became alive.

But what had really gone wrong was the constant nagging question before me. I must listen more carefully to what he is saying and what he is not saying. His life seems to be speaking, but he finds it hard to put into words—especially now when he is depressed, when so much of what he is experiencing is already blunted. His heart is so heavy.

As he slowly continued, it became very apparent that he was threatened by the "upcoming young bucks," as he called the younger executives who were being promoted. He saw his age as a very definite liability. It was obvious that in the forseeable future he would be replaced. The fact that he had earned a handsome retirement, aside from the many other excellent investments made no difference to his view of the future. He could not comprehend that he earned a well-deserved rest. This idea simply triggered panic and no hope at all.

The fact that he had been very successful gave him no comfort either. He had walked with the princes of the business world, and flown with the kings of them all. My calling this to his attention left no impression. Neither the memory of the past nor the hope of the future offered any consolation.

Soon another attribute of this man emerged. He was an absolute tyrant for perfection. He expected not one fraction of deviation from his norm, neither from himself, his children, nor his wife.

During his early years with the company his high performance goal for himself and for others resulted in his very quick rise up the ladder of the corporation. They all loved his productivity, his exactness, and promoted him for it. People under him responded or else they disappeared. "A valuable asset to the company," they said. "You deserve to be with the top echelon. You are good for the company."

An engulfing sadness crept through the room as we arrived at the mid-years of his life. These were the years of his greatest professional success, but, unfortunately, he carried this style of living with him wherever he went. His children all discovered a pattern of life to cope with such a powerful demanding father. The two girls married early and disappeared. The two boys learned a success model from the father. One was in medicine, the other in business, but they left for distant states to practice. None of the children or, now the grandchildren, came to see him except as it was part of "passing through this area."

His wife did not fare as well. The marriage lasted twenty-five years. Throughout this time she was quiet and submissive. She suffered silently, cleaned the house to his absolute demands, prepared his exact taste in food. Then, one day, someone showed her attention without any demands—the kind she never got at home. She, too, disappeared.

After that he had a series of mistresses who temporarily flew with him to a high lifestyle, but then soon discovered the price he exacted from them for this, and he lost touch with them all. Now he was alone.

Twenty years ago he should have been seeking help, I kept on thinking. That is when his life was screaming the most, but he didn't hear. He should have heard it from his meek wife, who suddenly could abandon all his wealth, comfort, and security just to escape what he was doing to her. The children's behavior was clear enough, but he was deaf to all of this. But why should he listen to his family when he was handed laurels on the job?

"Life has to be beat and bent to fit your style. When it resists, you strike all the harder until it gives; but I will not yield," was the motto of his life.

Now his message is beginning to come through. It is not what he is presently experiencing. He appears to have everything that man could desire. Then why all the despair?

I believe I hear his past screaming to be heard. So let's go on with his story.

I knew he had frequently alluded to the war years, but their significance had escaped me. He told me that he had flown a Spitfire, but said little else.

Then, one day he came to my office after a weekend meeting of the American Bonanza Society. He flew to a city in the midwest for this annual celebration of the many elite pilots from across the nation. As was their tradition, a group of pilots who fought in the "Battle of Britain" got together. It was an occasion to reminisce by telling and retelling all of their heroic experiences together.

As he told me this account, he became alive, pulsating with fiery enthusiasm. The entire office was filled with descriptive metaphors as he must have recounted only a few days previously. Suddenly, I was aware that herein lay a gold mine of information to understand this man. It was very apparent that this stage was when he was at the high point of his life.

He lived through the "Battle of Britain" in the cockpit of a Spitfire; every second counted. One false move and he would have been a war casualty as so many of his buddies had been. He told of one dog fight after another with the German Messerschmitts, and he was always the victor. Singlehandedly, he repeatedly approached the huge bomb-carrying plane, in the pitch blackness of the night over the English channel. Guns were blazing at him, yet he dared to dive right at the plane in counter attack. He made one approach after another until it dropped in flames to the water below. His absolute daredevil attitude was the talk of the home base. It was even a known fact that very few of his bunk-mates or fellow pilots made it, but he returned after each flight. He even volunteered for extra trips, as if to defy death. And yet he lived. He had the distinct feeling that he was destined to survive and that it was unrelated to chance. "Fate would have it be," he said.

As time went on he added up his casualties one by one. He was repeatedly decorated for heroism. Inside, though, a gradual awareness emerged that he was not heroic at all. It was that he was simply indestructible, no matter what chances he took.

As the war ended he received much acclaim, including personal invitations by high ranking men of the military and government. It was at this time, although he was only thirty years of age, that he was destined for glory, honor, fame, and fortune. He had only begun to experience the climb in life that would go on and on to heights far beyond man's highest imagination. If at this young an age all this was possible, then how much more was yet to come in thirty or forty years? He would simply live his life by the key lesson he had learned in the cockpit—absolute determination and self-control every second of time. There would be no room for human fallacy or error. He would expect perfection in performance from himself and from everyone else. By sheer force of will-power life would happen or he would make it happen.

At that very moment a light dawned within me. I am now hearing this man's past screaming in the midst of all the rubble.

No wonder he is in such despair. This man reached the crest of life at thirty years of age. Regardless of how much he beat and battered away at the system, it could never again give him what he once had. He could never attain anything near what he had once known. All the rest was below the summit and much of it downhill. Now, waiting for him was a deep valley that inwardly meant the worlds he was going to conquer were gone forever. The fantastic, unrealistic dream lay in shambles, and he lay slouched in my office weeping at the loss.

I could now hear this man had failed on a number of counts. He did not know that the mountaintop experience of his early twenties was in itself fantastic, but a very, very false introduction to life. He thought this experience was the launching pad for the remainder of life. The truth is he misunderstood this experience. It was really downhill all the way after that.

Although his later struggle to succeed had its rewards, it was only a desperate attempt to relive his earlier life. He was wrong in assuming that phenomenal achievements were his entitled reward. There is no such gift in life. Man is not destined to be great. It is out of the daily struggle, used correctly, that greatness can be achieved.

Life is not here to be managed. It must be lived in harmony with what is. Some parts must be changed, but much of it cannot be. There are times when yielding to the inevitable is the only course of action. Man is finite and he dare not ever forget that.

Albert never heard this message. When he imposed the message from "the Spitfire cockpit," his family fled from him. Now the "young bucks" were replacing him. His iron will took him through the war and gave him corporate success for a while, but little else.

Now he lay in utter despair, in a sad situation. His life could have been good, if not even great. With, theoretically, fifteen more good years to go and with the resources at his disposal, it could still be fruitful.

In his opinion, at this moment, it was no use trying. "It's too late," he said. And, if he is not willing or able to hear, it may well be too late.

The next stage in life is death. This can be extremely hard to face when one has not lived at all. How can one let go of something one has never claimed?

The fact that Alfred was entering the final stage of life in despair made him even wish it were all over because death appeared more desirable than despair.

It is a well-known fact that in this final stage a basic conflict emerges. It is the tension between sinking into despair or assuming a sense of integrity. To have integrity one must live through all of life's stages, so that one can finish each in its time and then let go of it and proceed to the next. Then, when the last period comes, one will feel a sense of completion. To defy the stages of the life process results in despair. That is a sad message at the end of life.

Listening with love to the entire experience of oneself or another can help bring closure to existence. This means that in looking back one makes a healthy summation in this manner: "It is the one life I had and I have lived it. At times I used all the resources and gifts available to me and made optimum use of them. At times I was foolish; I wasted occasions, lost great opportunities, or even destroyed the potentialities. I cannot live it over again. In light of this whole past pattern, I will now choose to use today and whatever tomorrows remaining to bring this life to an appropriate end."

Listening to older persons can help them bring closure to their lives. To accurately have one's life heard, as it was, gives one the occasion to make peace with the past.

I know of a young couple who discovered how to listen with love to their aged widowed mother. The difficulty occurred every year at Christmas time. The elderly lady purchased an endless quantity of gifts for children and grandchildren. Many months before Christmas she would send for large orders from the standard mail order as well as gadget catalogues. She insisted on going on repeated shopping trips to buy more and more gifts. That she was driven to do this by a motivation other than simple generosity was very apparent. When they attempted to stop her or reason with her she reacted with deep pain. To tell her that her income did not permit this type of excessive spending was of no value. When they limited her shopping trips, she simply ordered more by mail.

The young couple were struggling financially and were forced to limit their purchases. In relation to the children they wanted to teach them to appreciate the worth of gifts in terms of feelings that go with the giving instead of grasping for quantities. No matter how persistently they communicated this message, the children knew it would all be undone when grandmother arrived. And it was!

On Christmas day when she had to be brought for the usual festivities, she came with washbaskets full of gifts for everyone. Her face shone with glee when the children screamed with delight as though Santa Claus had, in fact, arrived in person. The atmosphere pervaded as the expensive gifts were opened. The fact that she was told that she should not have done it made her enjoy it all the more. At times the couple thought this was done out of spite, or even to show them how to celebrate Christmas.

One year, when all the commotion was over and the children had disappeared, she became very sullen. Then she began talking about her own childhood Christmas experience. Her father had been irresponsible, often unemployed, and usually so during the winter months. She knew when money was dwindling as the food became more and more sparse. If this happened before Christmas she knew that gifts would indeed be few. She remembered one year most vividly. Long before Christmas all trips to town ceased and only home-prepared items were served. This year she was sure that she would wake up Christmas morning only to discover there would be nothing. The fright was much more related to the fact of experiencing the shock, than it was what the gift would be. The next morning one tiny gift lay on the plate that she had set out the night before. In the package was a small booklet with proverbs on each page. She was greatly relieved, for there was something. Now she could express her gratitude to her parents. It was not until later in the day, as she was trying to determine how her parents could have bought it, that she realized that it had been purchased only the night before from a traveling peddler who happened to have passed by. Then she became overwhelmed with panic. Only by the coincidence of this man's passing through had she received a gift. Otherwise, there would have been nothing. An absolutely unbearable thought!

As she spoke a ghastly silence filled the room. Slowly she opened her purse and there she had the booklet. For more than seventy years she had kept it; still in perfect condition. It had rescued her from a disaster the size of which she even now could not comprehend.

The young couple said nothing, for nothing needed to be said. They all knew what she was saying. The message was loud and clear. They simply reviewed all the beautiful gifts she had given and expressed gratitude upon gratitude for all of them. She responded with a sense of fulfillment at having been understood.

They now knew that her Christmas behavior was not irrational. It was a desperate effort to heal her past by making absolutely certain that it would never happen to her descendants. The apparent excesses now only communicated the degree of her childhood agony, and that's all. In the future they would help her celebrate Christmas her way.

Lives can be understood if we only take time to listen. We are so ready to judge them from our vantage point. If we could only free people to share their lives with us, then we would understand. If we could reserve our opinion until we had walked miles in their moccasins, as the Indian saying states it. The elderly need to be heard this way.

Listening with love will help take the total span of

existence and bring it together into a meaningful whole. Then, when death comes, life will not be torn away, but rather it can be freely surrendered because it is finished.

8

CINDY
When Listening with Love Transforms

Most people we meet do not accept themselves as unique, special or, may I even say, precious. After all, that is what every human being really is. For many the traumas—the rejections—of early childhood have left an indelible impression. As a result they now hate themselves. Deep inside their feelings are screaming to them that they are worthless. Even worse, they feel like they are defective products of the human assembly line.

Since this is how they experience themselves, they are also very ashamed of themselves. So they spend their lives hiding their true selves from all outsiders. To expose this inner world would publicly reveal their self-perceived deficiencies. Since they already feel bad about themselves, this would make it even worse. And so they crawl deeper into themselves.

Mrs. Rice—Cindy—is a perfect illustration of an individual with this type of degrading self-image. Her early family situation had the exact destructive drama to create such a total negative self-image. Cindy's mother criticized her every move relentlessly; Mother always knew best.

Cindy's father was a gentle, long-suffering man, but he constantly received the same kind of verbal abuse as Cindy. By the time she was five, Cindy's father was

CINDY: *When Listening with Love Transforms*

well on the road to alcoholism, driven there by the incessant attacks on his masculinity and humanity by Cindy's mother who then blamed him for all the family suffering.

Each night, totally drunk, Cindy's father heaped hour after hour of abusive, violent, and sexually obscene language upon the family. He cursed Cindy's mother and older brother endlessly. He cursed God, the politicians, their relatives, everyone in the world except Cindy, his "dolly." The more he cursed her mother and brother, the more they resented, rejected, and ridiculed Cindy.

Cindy came out of this ordeal a loser. She was deeply scarred. She arrived at adulthood with violent self-hatred which was focused mainly on her physical appearance. Her mother had spent many hours over the years telling her how ugly and unlovable she was. Because of the shabby, inappropriate, and ill-fitting clothes her mother made her wear, Cindy's peer group defined her as "ugly and weird" and rejected her also. She took these messages as a true picture of herself and repudiated herself.

The only person in all this who really cared for Cindy was her father, the alcoholic. His valuing of her could not stand up to the pressure of family and peer group, but it was that kernel of love which gave Cindy the strength to survive those years.

With only her father's encouragement, Cindy became an excellent scholar. Her father urged her to attend college and thereby won a royal battle in his marriage, perhaps the only one. Cindy was sent out of the house and out of the area to college—away from the oppressive, denigrating influence of her mother and brother.

At college she shone like a star in the university classes and in the sorority that cherished her membership. For the first time ever Cindy lived a spontaneous and joyous existence. Now she was totally free from the negative barbs tossed at her all her life.

All went very well for her for a while. She courted and married a most enviable campus brain. He greatly adored her and adorned her. But the deep secrets of her heart remained inaccessible to both of them. The scars of the past could not be exposed.

Then, on the day of the delivery of her first child, all of her self-repulsion erupted like a volcano. She could not accept that her defective body could produce a normal child, and in labor came to believe the child would be born dead.

As she cared for the baby, she began to behave toward the child as her mother had behaved toward her. She saw that this child would be condemned to endure the childhood she had endured and she would become her mother whom she hated.

Her world caved in. She went into a deep depression, not sure whether to kill the child, or herself, or both. All that she had always believed about herself could no longer be hidden. It simply engulfed her in utter despair.

At that point, she and her husband came to me for help. They could no longer live this way. Her fear of the counseling experience was great, for I might confirm that she was after all worthless, if not mentally ill. In her mind I might join the mocking crowd of her childhood, although I would not.

It was very easy to listen with love to her deepest heart's desire. She was screaming to be rescued from

CINDY: *When Listening with Love Transforms*

the destructive self-condemnation that was engraved into her soul. I would not pick up the theme of her mother, nor of her childhood peers, but rather I responded to all the beauty of personhood that had also been forged in the midst of all this suffering. Soon she also learned to listen with love to herself. There was no crowd jeering her, but she was only mocking herself. She had, in fact, been her own worst enemy. She dumped an enormous amount of accusations on her husband. He was on her side, but her feelings of lack of unworthiness were deflecting from him.

Out of all this, a young mother emerged who could suddenly stand tall for the world to see. She discovered her talents and with great freedom and skill could exercise them.

As this was going on, a neighbor who was caring for her child while she kept her clinic appointment, began to ask what was happening in treatment. This friend knew she was being helped and wanted an explanation. "What, in fact, happens in such an experience?"

Cindy did not want to reveal the data of this experience. For her neighbor to really understand she would need to tell a lot about her family that she did not care for anyone to know. It would impair their relationship. Suddenly, it occurred to her that she could use an analogy to tell the entire experience without telling any facts. With my encouragement this account was written to share with others.

It is as if I were dwelling in a great big old house, which I haven't shown to anyone. I am so ashamed of what it looks like inside. People would laugh if they saw it. I'm scared of what they would say about it after-

ward, so I let no one inside. It's been a long time that I have kept my door closed and my drapes pulled.

People used to knock, but they don't any more.

They gave up!

Then, one day I could not take the loneliness any more. I called this man, about whom I had heard many a kind thing.

"Please, please, come over. I can no longer live in this place, and I can't get out."

And he did—immediately—much to my surprise.

I met him at the gate, where he stopped to talk. He was in no hurry to go any farther.

Apparently he will let me guide the way in. And he will let me set the pace.

I noticed his delicate hands as he fondled the weather-beaten wood in the gate and then added, "The rain and the storms have carved this wood like no craftsman could."

I had never noticed. All I knew was that it badly needed repairing. "How could he see beauty in that?" I thought.

It seemed so natural to invite him back next week.

Before I knew it, we were sitting together on the garden swing. "This gives us a good view of the house," he said. He is so observant and so sensitive.

We soon noticed the garden paths. We reflected about the many little feet that must have trodden there.

I began to reminisce about the past, how I as a child had played here. This swing was especially dear to me.

He took everything inside himself that I said, and kept it as if it were a treasure.

I knew he wanted to know more and more, but he did not rush me.

He knew I needed time.

CINDY: *When Listening with Love Transforms*

Then later we sat on the porch. From here he observed the lattice work. He admired the craftsman who spent many long hours fashioning it.

"It's mine," I thought; and I never knew I had anything that precious.

He is so kind, so gentle. I long for him when he is not here. I thought far too much of him. I even sat where he had sat, and searched for the beauty that he could see.

I would have been ashamed had anyone known that I was doing this, but then, no one could know. They never came by anymore.

Then one day when he came again, I had the urge to invite him in.

I should have been afraid, but I wasn't.

I should have been ashamed, but I couldn't be.

He made all of that so different.

For a moment I panicked and said I shouldn't do this.

He seemed hurt by what I said. I heard him mumble quietly, "Shoulds and should nots—people have so many of those and they keep on hanging more and more around each other's neck, until someone's back bends. Someday you will be relieved of this burden."

I was startled, "But I need them to guide my life."

"Yes," he said kindly, "I know you do now, but not always. You will find a guide within yourself some day. But I will never make you do anything you don't want to do. We both know you need to give them up in time to come."

Then I asked him to step in. "Yes," he replied, "It's time now."

Once inside he looked around very carefully. He noticed everything. Nothing appeared hidden from his gaze.

Then he exclaimed in childlike wonder, "Oh my! How precious! How beautiful!"

He picked up a vase that had stood on a shelf by the door for years. He handled it delicately as he remarked, "It is pure China."

As he set it down, it became precious to me.

"I'm going to keep it," I said.

"Yes, you had better. It will be worth a lot to you some day," he replied.

The visits at first were far too brief. So I asked him to come back again and again.

Until now the house was always dark. It felt good that way.

One day he went to the drapes as if to open them for the first time in years and years. But he stopped short as he touched them and said, "Velvet."

"I never noticed," I exclaimed as I rushed to his side. With that I tore the drapes open, and sure enough, bright, red velvet that glistened in the sunlight.

"And look at the rug," he gushed forth. In no time we were down on our knees feeling it as he breathed softly, "It's Turkish!"

"But I thought . . ." I tried to say, but he quickly added, "and hardly ever used. It's precious."

"It's old and ugly and I hate it," I said, and I told him how it had come to be in the house—through the greed and selfishness of others. "Someday I'll throw it out for the trashmen!"

"If you dislike it, it's okay to get rid of it," he said. But then he showed me the intricacies of its weaving and helped me to understand its value.

"If you want to be rid of it, that's fine," he said, "but don't give it away. Sell it for what it's really worth."

I was relieved. I knew he would not force me or steal from me, as others had. And he understood my feelings.

For the next many weeks we went through the whole house. Slowly, we explored it, room after room, with all the excitement and wonder that only he could create. I noticed that he was especially delicate as we entered each room.

Every room changed as we visited it.

Often during the day I returned to those rooms on my own and kept on exploring for myself. It always felt like he was with me.

I could even hear his exclamation, "Beautiful." That is his favorite one. The way he said it made me feel the beauty.

"And why," I kept on saying to myself, "hadn't anyone told me before? I have lived here in darkness so long."

Almost all of my waking hours I spent with this strange venture, exploring my house. It was so hard to believe that this was the same old house.

"How could it change so much?"

The old rocking chair in the nursery became my favorite. It had been here long before I was born. It was my favorite in early childhood. I know I sat there for many hours clutching my teddy bear, rocking myself, and sucking my thumb. One time as I held onto that same teddy bear a strange chill went through my body. "That was weird," I thought. "I will ask him why this was so, when he comes again."

He was very careful when he answered that question. He knew it was delicate. I soon knew that long ago I had been alone and cold far too much when I should have been warmly cuddled. In those days they just didn't know what little ones needed. The warmth I should have had just wasn't available.

So I was left alone in the cold.

Then he added, "Whenever you have those sad re-

minders just let them be, because they, too, are a part of you."

After many visits to that room of my childhood, and many, many long conversations, the room became more and more cozy. I then asked him if I may sleep here tonight. He said that it would be all right.

So I slept there!

I slept soundly and I had a beautiful dream. "How strange," I mused to myself in the morning, "I had so many nightmares when I slept here before. And of all the places to have such a restful night."

We made the rounds, over and over again. It was all very nice, but I could tell he was looking for something else. As time went on his eyes became more and more searching.

Then one day he clasped my hands in his, and held on tightly until he knew I was secure.

He suddenly asked, "Where is the closet?"

"What closet?" I exclaimed.

"You know," he said softly but very firmly.

"Oh, no! Do we have to?"

"Yes!" he said, even more firmly. The hurt showed in his eyes. I know he would have avoided it if he could have, but he couldn't. It was necessary.

I had not let myself think of that closet, although I was always aware that it was there.

Only once did it cross my mind, that he might ask to see it. But then I dismissed it like I always did before. Only at night, when I couldn't sleep, did it come back to me, and I was unable to wipe it from my mind.

Then, at times, in my nightmares the door flung open. It scared me so that I woke up screaming. For days I had that awful haunted feeling.

"Why does this same nightmare come back again and again?" I asked him.

CINDY: *When Listening with Love Transforms*

"*Because no one has ever taken you by the hand and taken you to that closet and helped you experience again what went wrong in this house so long ago. It has remained a mystery long enough. Where is it?*" *he asked.*

"*Don't let go of my hand and I will take you there.*"

So we went into a small room and there, hidden in a dark corner, was the door.

I simply pointed, as he led the way.

As he took a hold of the door, he said, "You know we have to."

"*Yes," I said, "I trust you. I know you knew what you were doing thus far, so I must trust you in this, too. I also know I cannot live here forever without knowing what that closet means. So please go ahead. I had hoped for so long that it would go away, but it didn't. And if I only could be rescued from those awful nightmares.*"

Then he added, "You know I already know what is in here."

"*But how can you?*"

"*Because the many other houses I have visited have always had one. And we always had to visit it before we stopped coming.*"

He opened it only a little the first day. He looked around very carefully.

"*Close it," he said. "It's OK. That is enough for today.*"

I made up my mind then that the next week I would take the lead and go directly to the closet and I would open the door.

So I did. I threw it wide open.

"*Let's get it over with," I screamed.*

He looked around carefully, with his alert eyes. I thought he was startled and that scared me.

He turned to me, and said with great compassion,

"Oh, I feel so sorry for you. So many and they have been here so long."

There we sat on the floor, before the open closet door, week after week, talking about all the horrible things that had happened to me, the many times I was so terribly frightened and humiliated. That is when this closet was filled with all my terrors.

This closet had a lot to tell us. We carefully learned the lessons it had to teach us. It is here that we discovered why I chose to hide in this house in the first place, why I became so ashamed, and why I hated it so much.

And so we disposed of everything that was in the closet. Then one day when the job was all done, together we closed the door, never again to fear it.

Together we casually strolled through the house again. I had the strange sensation that it no longer resembled the one I used to live in.

It all had become new.

It was so bright and airy.

On the days when he was not with me, I would do many unusual things. Some seem silly to tell. I ran, skipped, and somersaulted, just for the pure joy of it.

The house was no longer a bondage to me; it was a delight to live in. And just to think it really is the same house, even older now.

How could this be?

All that happened was that I asked someone to visit me.

I let someone in and it all changed.

It has been many years since he last came, but by now I have had many other people over, and I have gone to see them. We have mutually explored each other's houses.

CINDY: *When Listening with Love Transforms* 169

Although they are all so very, very different, we have so much that resembles each other. We have agreed that they must have been built by one builder.

Soon after this Mrs. Rice and her husband returned to her distant home community for the tenth anniversary of her high school class graduation. For the occasion she dressed in a formal fitted floor length gown in a deep blue satin. She made it herself. This was extremely significant since it was this very body, in this same audience, which had caused her deep trauma so long ago. The super clique was running the show as they had done with such power years ago. But they had never left the little mountain community, nor had they discovered the world beyond the ridges. Instead, they married early and succumbed to a very mediocre existence with many children. They, too, took upon themselves the privilege of awarding honors upon the class for many achievements. Some received awards for the most children, for the most original outfit, etc. Much to Cindy's astonishment she was awarded the prize for "the person who had changed the most."

There was no question in the minds of these hundreds of classmates that she was the ugly duckling who graduated with them, but returned the much envied swan. This was a transformation that no one could comprehend. If they could only have known that it was the absence of their love that had crippled her so long ago. It was love that listened to her crying heart and transformed her later.

Listening with love transforms what it loves. To listen totally means that one takes another's whole life into one's being and cares for it.

When I listen with love I open myself, my life to

another person. I ask him to come in just as he is. No disguising is necessary with me. Now, for once, he need not put on a mask or distort anything. I say to him that he is a unique human being and that I will value all he can entrust to me. He can now fully reveal his inner world and I will receive the whole person by listening. The door to his inner world is his words—his own description of how he experiences it. My door to entering that world is by listening. When this is done something very meaningful happens.

An interpersonal transaction of this depth can happen only if it is done with love. It is far too risky for anyone to expose his inner life unless he has the absolute assurance that it will be used solely for his good. Love is the only guarantee one can give. It is when I really operate on the law of ultimate love that I can give someone the assurance that I will do nothing else with his life but what is for his greatest welfare.

People intuitively measure the depth of love of all persons in all interpersonal relationships. If love is felt to be genuine, they will reveal much. If it is lacking, they will remain superficial. If they sense malice in the listener's heart, then they will say nothing important. They may even disguise and distort what they say so as to protect themselves from being mutilated by what they are sharing. But love opens the way to the full depth of another person.

Love will never hurt what it loves. Another person's ultimate good is the lover's final goal. With love as the dominating motivation in life, one goes down to the hurt, the agony, the deformity of another human being in order to heal, to correct, to bring comfort.

In listening, love has to be assured, or it is not really listening. It must liberate the speaker to unveil everything without any need to sort out what is appropriate. Everything that needs to be said will be said. It will all be held gently by the listener, to support the fact that it is very, very precious. It is, after all, another human being's life.

In actual practice, listening with love is an art. I find it expedient to be constantly communicating my caring to the one who is talking. At times it need only be a simple affirmation like, "Yes, I see"; or "Go on, I am with you"; but my voice must carry the empathy.

At times it is necessary to restate the words that I hear to convey the assurance that I heard it all.

On other occasions it is more appropriate to ask for more feelings, with expressions like "My, that must have been painful!" or "How could you endure it?" or simply, "Oh! That is beautiful."

Then there are times when the speaker cannot put into words his own heart's cry. It is blatantly obvious to me so I will respond cautiously with, "What I hear you saying is. . . ." Then I pick up all the parts of the many sentences, as if they are pieces from a jigsaw puzzle, and with the help of the individual I put them together. This can bring about a startling revelation or insight that was not known before.

Listening at this level is a creative act. It means that the fragmented pieces of a person are brought together into a single meaningful whole. A new life is born at that moment.

At times this is a frightening experience. The person may never have known that his life was screaming a message that he could not dare let himself hear. Now, finally, it is out in the open. It has been said and someone heard it.

Sometimes it is a very pleasant surprise. The words

one is saying are brought together into a single whole. It is exactly what he has been yearning to do, and accurate listening did it for him.

Is this not transformation?

There is healing power in listening. As a speaker unveils the deepest hidden material to me, he discovers that I deeply cherish all of it. Then, he gradually cares about it too. He now takes back that which he has given to me to hold temporarily.

At times it is just that part of himself which was so unbearable to him, so disgusting or even shameful, that he claims as his uniqueness. It is now a special part of his experience. Because I valued it while I held it, he now values it too. He comes out of this experience a marvelous human being equal to, although vastly different from, every other human being. This is exactly what every person has the right to claim.

He has discovered his distinctive difference, whatever that may be, and loves it because I loved it first. Only months earlier, he came into my presence ashamed, dejected, or severely depressed. Now he leaps for joy as he tells himself, "I am indeed a unique creature marvelously put together out of all of life's agonies and ecstasies. That is what makes me be me, just like it makes everyone else be themselves."

When someone has found the key to relationship—the principle of listening with love—he has a new tool to reach out to others. Much to his own amazement, it works for him also. He finds that people are not shunning him because of his ugliness, but because they fear revealing their own feelings of inner ugliness. Now as he extends his hand in love to others, people respond, much to his surprise. They also have long been waiting, in the shadows, for someone to come along with a gentle

CINDY: *When Listening with Love Transforms* 173

hand, a tender heart, a sensitive soul, and open ears. As they mutually share their inner fears nonjudgmentally, they discover a kinship that they have not known before, and the power of transforming love spreads.

Let us go back to Cindy's analogy. Her house became haunted long ago, as a child, when she shared her inner experience with her parents and they did not respond in love. What she did give them, they mutilated, and she learned not to give anymore. Then she became estranged from her own feelings, from her own experience of herself. Since so much criticism was focused on her appearance, her self-hatred became lodged in her body. She got a brief relief through her sorority and her suitor. But she could not share her inner dwelling even with these people. It was too frightening for her to enter.

Then, at the moment of greatest vulnerability, all the skeletons in the closet came rushing out, and she disintegrated. After this the miraculous law of listening with love was put to a test. Cindy was transformed. She was made whole.

You have met Joanne, me, Kathy, Jim, Linda, Joe, Melissa, Albert and Cindy. But then there are Frank, Jerry, Martha, and dozens more in your life waiting to be heard and healed.

A divine act of listening with love two thousand years ago transformed the history of mankind. An author, Paul, who had personally experienced this change said it more eloquently than I could:

If I had the gift of being able to speak in other languages without learning them, and could speak in every language there is in all of heaven and earth, but didn't love others, I would only be making noise. If I had the gift of prophecy and knew all about what is going to happen in the future, knew everything about everything, *but didn't love others, what good would it do? Even if I had the gift of faith so that I could speak to a mountain and make it move, I would still be worth nothing at all without love. If I gave everything I have to poor people, and if I were burned alive for preaching the Gospel but didn't love others, it would be of no value whatever.*

Love is very patient and kind, never jealous or envious, never boastful or proud, never haughty or selfish or rude. Love does not demand its own way. It is not irritable or touchy. It does not hold grudges and will hardly even notice when others do it wrong. It is never glad about injustice, but rejoices whenever truth wins out. If you love someone you will be loyal to him no matter what the cost. You will always believe in him, always expect the best of him, and always stand your ground in defending him. . . . There are three things that remain—faith, hope, and love—and the greatest of these is love (1 Cor. 13:1–7, 13 TLB*).*